Lowell Metzler

5-27-88
4-16-90

BIRTHDAY FROM
FAMILY

Laughter, Joy,
and Healing

Laughter, Joy, and Healing

Donald E. Demaray

BAKER BOOK HOUSE
Grand Rapids, Michigan 49506

The book is affectionately dedicated
to my grandchildren
Christopher
Kathleen
Matthew
Shawn
who are ready for a good laugh
most of the time

It must never be forgotten that joy is one of the commonest New Testament words.

—William Barclay

It is the heart that is unsure of his God that is afraid to laugh.

—George MacDonald

Contents

Preface

This book, without question, is the most exciting I have undertaken. To learn that laughter and joy can actually alter moods and often bring physical healing—well, that good news turned me on. One authority even goes so far as to say that if you laugh less than fifteen times daily, including three belly laughs, you are "underlaughed."

Norman Cousins calls laughing "internal jogging." Humor sends pleasure coursing through our thought processes, assists in reestablishing perspective, opens our minds to new vistas of reality, and releases us from tension. Spiritually, it restores faith—a major purpose of this book—and thus plays its role in making prayer and creative living real and meaningful. It is no accident that "Praying Hyde," that spiritual dynamo behind one of the most effective Christian awakenings in India, was known not only for the impact of his intercessions but also for the hilarity of his laugh.

William F. Fry, Stanford University psychiatrist and longtime student of laughter, believes that virtually all body systems are influenced by humor. Heart muscles, circulation, lungs, respiration, alertness hormones, brain and central nervous system—all, it seems, thereby undergo therapy. Moreover, we know that negative emotions like fear and anger, as well as depression, can be modified through laughter. Fry calls laughter the royal road to the subconscious.

Yet one looks almost in vain for references to humor-

and-joy therapy in health handbooks and spiritual guides. Perhaps that is because only recently have the health communities looked upon humor as a serious instrument of healing. True, through the centuries, doctors, counselors, and ministers have intuited laughter's part in wholeness, and references may be found on the relation of hope and healing. But widespread study is recent, probably prompted by Norman Cousins's now-historic autobiographical article in the *New England Journal of Medicine* (December 23, 1976), reprinted in *Reader's Digest* and *Saturday Review*. It took revised form in Cousins's book, *The Anatomy of an Illness*, a work that spelled out at some length and in helpful detail the implications of laughter as a metaphor for positivity and faith and showed its power as a means of restoring health.

My aim is to help people in the struggle of life to rise to overcoming and productive faith. Since daily challenges make us busy people, I have designed this book for easy reading and reflection. The readings, one for each day over a thirteen-week period—in other words, a quarter of a year— require only five or six minutes, not even that in some cases. But all are designed to inspire and inform. Motifs, each time seen through fresh lenses, make clear and permanent some principles often overlooked but essential for wholeness and meaningful living.

Donald E. Demaray

Acknowledgments

For all those who have made my research and writing possible, and to others who have assisted in advancing this project, I am grateful. I express thanks to Dr. Kenneth Kinghorn, provost of Asbury Theological Seminary at the time I began the manuscript, and to Dr. Melvin Dieter, present provost. To Dr. David McKenna, president of the seminary, who has encouraged and suggested, I owe further appreciation. Nor can I forget faculty colleagues, most particularly Dr. Fred Layman, who took time to chat and point me to helpful books and articles. I wish also to thank the seminary's Faculty Research Committee, administration, and board of trustees for giving permission for my sabbatical, without which the book could not have come to birth.

The libraries that provided sources of information include the following: The British Museum, London, where I always find a happy and eager assistance; I am grateful for reading-room assistance across the years. The public library in Pietermaritzburg, South Africa, along with the resources of the Evangelical Biblical Seminary of Southern Africa, also in Pietermaritzburg, deserve recognition. The Asbury Theological Seminary library—especially Mrs. Eunice Weldon, a research librarian, along with research assistants John Seery and Dorothy James—provided aid as often as requested, and always with joy. The community library in North Myrtle Beach, South Carolina, as well as the Myrtle Beach Library, gave me assistance. The central public library at Lexington, Kentucky, provided further help.

To my wife, Kathleen, and my father, C. Dorr Demaray, for manuscript reading and counsel, I express my thanks. For my children, Cherith, Elyse, and James, and the grandchildren, Matthew, Kathleen, Shawn, and Christopher, I owe a special debt of gratitude, as I do my son-in-law, Paul Davenport, and my daughter-in-law, Charlene Demaray, for the rich resources of family life and ongoing humor they make available. Martin Luther believed the family was the laboratory of life learning; he was so right.

I must also thank Harriet Norris, former head faculty secretary at Asbury Seminary, for her administrative assistance, and Brook Thelander, who put the manuscript on the word processor and typed revisions.

Finally, I cannot forget to thank Baker Book House staff for helps through the years, too numerous to mention, and also for permission to quote from my 1983 book, *Watch Out for Burnout*.

Laughter Therapy

I was greatly elated by the discovery that there is a physiological basis for the ancient theory that laughter is good medicine.

—Norman Cousins

1

The Scientific Practice
of Laughter

"A cheerful heart is a good medicine," says the writer of Proverbs, "but a downcast spirit dries up the bones" (Prov. 17:22). Norman Cousins, whose laughter-and-healing discoveries are now taught in a number of medical colleges, discovered for himself the wisdom outlined in the Book of Proverbs. Cousins tells his story in some detail in the celebrated 1979 volume, *Anatomy of an Illness as Perceived by the Patient: Reflections on Healing and Regeneration.* His story in summary goes like this:

In August 1964 Cousins flew home from overseas, suffering some fever and dull pain. Within a few days he could move neck, arms, hands, fingers, and legs only with difficulty. Tests showed he suffered a collagen disease (collagen is the fibrous material holding cells together). "In a sense, then, I was coming unstuck," says Cousins. "Nodules appeared on my body, gravel-like substances under the skin. . . ." His chances for recovery, according to the doctors? One in 500!

Taking initiative with the support and guidance of his doctors, Cousins studied the medical literature and discovered he was suffering adrenal exhaustion brought on by tension, that negative emotions had changed his body chemistry for the worse. Naturally he wondered whether positive thought could alter this chemistry for the better. He was soon to get his answer. But first he found that nearly all medicines given him in the hospital acted as blockages to healing. Apparently what he needed was to get his endocrine system functioning properly; that is, to get his immune powers to combat the disease. Cousins now proceeded to experiment. And he made significant breakthroughs.

His firsthand detective work taught him that faith, the will to live, hope—in other words, an upbeat attitude—correlated directly to pain reduction. Cousins also traced the vitamin C connection—massive doses really helped—though surely as important was his frame of mind. Refusing to get caught in the trap of hopelessness, he engineered a program of laughter. Funny movies, hilarious stories, and the determination to laugh instead of cry brought him to an amazing realization: ". . . ten minutes of genuine belly laughter had an anesthetic effect and would give me at least two hours of pain-free sleep." Sedimentation-rate testing proved that his laughter episodes not only produced lowered sed-rate readings at the time, but that the whole merriment procedure yielded a cumulative benefit. He was getting well. "I was greatly elated by the discovery that there is a physiological basis for the ancient theory that laughter is good medicine," Norman Cousins concluded. He recovered.

2

Laughter as Healing Friend

"A cheerful heart," says the biblical writer, "has a continual feast" (Prov. 15:15b). Norman Cousins met another physical challenge in 1980, more than a decade and a half after winning over the collagen disease. He tells all in *The Healing Heart: Antidotes to Panic and Helplessness* (1983).

Cousins, for a long time far too busy with lecturing and touring to satisfy his body's requirements for exercise and rest, suffered a massive heart attack. Poor diet had also contributed to his health problems.

Wisely, he refused to panic. Panic, he had observed, constricts the blood vessels. So, calm and confident, he instructed the ambulance driver not to turn on the siren, to drive at normal speed—in a word, to defuse the mood of emergency. In this way, he testifies, the trip to the hospital spared him the usual "strenuous heroics."

As professor of medical humanities at the University of California at Los Angeles School of Medicine, Cousins tells doctors and medical technologists to recognize that when people are confronted by physical crisis, "Reassurance is the first order of treatment," not histrionics. ". . . de-escalate the usual emergency mood" is his wise instruction.

Once in the hospital setting, Cousins asked for the same unagitated treatment, including no waking him in the night for medication. This he worked out with his doctor. But his physician leveled with Cousins: "No laughing. You yourself have said laughing is a form of internal jogging. You're not up to any jogging right now. . . . Stay flat on your back and just be a vegetable." Cousins wondered if his condition was worse than the doctor had earlier intimated.

Shortly after this "lecture," his wife, Ellen, entered the hospital room. Norman reported the doctor's orders—no laughing, "something I had little practice in doing. . . ." But Mrs. Cousins read the day's issue of *The Los Angeles Times* to her husband, and one of the stories was so funny that he let out a great roar of laughter, causing nurses to come running. As it turned out, the mirth had done no damage at all. "Right then, I knew I was going to make it all the way. Laughter was still a friend."

3

The Therapeutic Power of a Laughfest

The apostle Paul put his finger on a thoroughly practical life principle when he said from his prison cell, "Rejoice in the Lord always; again I will say, Rejoice" (Phil. 4:4). But the law he so succinctly articulated must not be interpreted naively. Newspaper accounts of Cousins's healing left the impression that he had laughed his way through and out of illness. Cousins himself observed, however, that thoughtful readers of his material knew laughter was "a metaphor for the entire range of positive emotions." He lists those emotions: hope, faith, love, the will to live, cheer, humor, creativity, playfulness, confidence, great expectations. The bottom line was that positive thoughts form the launching pad for getting well.

One is reminded of the psychologist Thomas W. Allen, a professor at Washington University (St. Louis), who says: "Our thoughts reverberate in our bodies." That means that for every positive thought there is a corresponding positive physiological reaction for the good.

Cousins, aware of the current move toward organized laughfests in hospitals as a factor in enhancing the curative effects of medical therapies, took on an assignment at the Sepulveda Veterans Administration Hospital in California. At the first meeting about half a hundred people assembled. Cousins reviewed brain-research findings, focusing on glandular activity. He went on to detail some benefits of laughing—William Fry, Jr., of Stanford's School of Medicine had itemized these benefits, including bettered respiration. Laughter builds a roadblock to panic and apprehension and frees up the body's healing systems, Cousins concluded.

After presenting his stimulating thoughts, Cousins engaged patients, along with doctors and nurses, in an experiment. They would create an atmosphere of laughter. And laugh they did. They laughed at stories and jokes; they laughed during the playing of a cassette laugh track. Contagion set in, and the audible mirth could hardly be stopped. After ten minutes, Cousins asked how they felt. For some, pain had lessened, showing perhaps that the body's endorphins, or natural pain killers, were at work.

The next step was a natural: the patients would set up their own programs of joke sharing, comedians on video—anything and everything to get people to laugh. The patients cooperated to the extent that a fellowship of participation was established, and this opened the door to weekly progress reports. The laughfest meetings pleased the physicians, not only because of the changed mood of the patients, but also because of their actual physical improvement.

4

Doctors Prescribe Laughter

Jesus, the Great Physician, declared the intended result of His teachings: ". . . that my joy may be in you, and that your joy may be full" (John 15:11). Part of that joy may well be a spirit of mirth.

Mark Twain intuited what modern science is now documenting. In *Tom Sawyer*, he tells about the old man who "laughed loud and joyously, shook up the details of his anatomy from head to foot, and ended by saying that such a laugh was 'money in a man's pocket, because it cut down the doctor's bills like everything.'"

A researcher for the Nurses for Laughter organization discovered that humorous nurses lend a sense of well-being to patients, speed up their adjustment to the hospital setting, and drain off worry. No wonder laughter programs are emerging in hospitals, and doctors are actually prescribing mirth.

Johns Hopkins Hospital shows humorous films—from "Candid Camera," the Three Stooges, whatever—on closed-circuit TV. Patients at Wilcox Memorial in Hawaii enjoy the benefits of stand-up comics who make videos; these professionals do their work *gratis*. At a Catholic hospital in Texas, nuns are assigned to tell funny stories to every patient on a daily basis!

Today, clowns go into mental hospitals and cancer wards

and also perform before cardiac patients. Some patients actually undergo cure, cancer victims enter recession periods, and the general tone of well-being rises. Some health-care and social-work professionals will now pay over two hundred dollars to register for a conference or workshop on laughter and play.

What is actually flowering in the literature and lecturing on play and fun is that life itself requires the jocular. Without glee, we are incomplete as human beings. Adults often lose this ability, even feel guilty about engaging in it. ("I really ought to be doing something more important," we reason.)

The *Seattle Times* (May 21, 1983) summed it up nicely: "Health professionals have long known that play and positive attitudes can help heal. In recent years, scientists also have begun to document the complex chemical changes that occur in the body as a result of both pleasure and stress." And, as far back as 1977, *The Indianapolis Star* (October 30) carried a tiny article entitled "Laugh Yourself to Health." "Doctors report increasing evidence," the piece began, "that a person can laugh himself to health." The article continues: "The November issue of Science Digest cites several studies in which laughter produced beneficial physical and mental results." Moreover, "A hearty laugh benefits lungs and clears the respiratory system," the researchers said.

5

A Safety Valve

Gerald Piaget, one of the founders of the Institute for the Advancement of Human Behavior and a professor of psychiatry at Stanford University, says humor that exposes the incongruities of life can provide safety valves for conflict. Moreover, the Laughter Project at the University of California, Santa Barbara, carried out research that showed laughter reduced stress just as efficiently as expensive biofeedback training. Try to beat that! No fees for a program, no equipment or lab—just the merriment that human beings can generate.

Hans Selye, father of modern stress research, documented chemical and biological factors in tension-oriented situations—adrenal enlargement, weight loss, increase of corticoids in the blood, and so on. All activity, he found, has a corresponding physiological response. This great Canadian doctor learned that adrenal exhaustion can erupt from emotional involvements such as frustration, disappointment, hidden and suppressed angers. However, he went on to find that this kind of energy depletion is really *dis*tress—stress itself is good, because it forms the launching pad for getting things done.

So the practical question emerges: How can I live with wholesome stress and avoid distress? The *Wellness Letter* of the University of California, Berkeley, gives us an answer in one long but delightful sentence: "Certainly a good, old-fashioned thigh-slapper can be a real workout, raising body temperature about a half a degree, setting the whole cardio-vascular system pulsating, throwing the abdominal, lumbar, internal intercostal, sub-costal, and transverse thoracic muscles into gear, rocking the glottis and larynx, rumbling up the windpipe, and banging against the trachea to emerge, finally, in a burst of mirth that sometimes issues from a person at a speed of 70 miles an hour, followed by muscle relaxation." That finding agrees with what Norman Cousins learned in the 1960s; namely, that ten minutes of belly laughter gave him two hours of pain-free sleep. Moreover, hilarity issues in muscle contraction in abdomen, chest, shoulders; heart, res-piration, and blood-pressure rates increase. After the laugh-ter episodes, muscles relax more than before, and heart and blood-pressure pace dip even below "normal."

Proverbs 12:25 hits the nail on the head: "Anxiety in a man's heart weighs him down, but a good word makes him glad." The safety valve of laughter has a way of releasing us to gladness and restoring normalcy.

6
Endorphins and All That

Jesus said we should "be of good cheer" (John 16:33). The good cheer He made possible writes itself into our very bodies. An American Medical Association bulletin carried the research finding that every organ of the body responds to laughter—reacts to the good!

In a telling article in *American Health,* Robert Brody details the body's response to a good hee-haw. The pituitary gland shoots out endorphins, chemical cousins of such painkilling drugs as heroin and morphine. The lacrimal glands of the eyes produce tears. The zygomatic muscles in the head contort as if in pain. The lower jaw vibrates lickety-bang. The arteries relax after tensing. Vocal cords undergo spasm and produce sound. The heart increases its pace, meeting immediate oxygen needs. Lungs build pressure before releasing air. The diaphragm tightens for spasms of respiration. From the nervous system comes a deluge of adrenaline, which issues in euphoria. Abdominal muscles double like a fist. Leg muscles relax, causing a weakening feeling.

Science (by the way, the study of laughter is known as gelotology—Greek *gelos* for "laughter")—is only in the preliminary stages of isolating laughter's benefits. But we already suspect that such pain-oriented diseases as arthritis can benefit; we know for a fact that both mental pain, such as depression, and physical distress may be reduced in some cases, that blood flow can be enhanced, that digestion can improve.

Dr. William F. Fry, Jr., a leading gelotologist of our time, reveals that laughter initiates "a massive brain reaction." Fry also learned that happy people may laugh up to four hundred times a day. Put that all together and see that the physical and psychological catharsis induced by hearty mirth helps explain the peace and good health many people enjoy.

7

A College Dedicated to Laughter

Clowns make us laugh, and laughter relieves stress. The Barnum and Bailey Clown College in Venice, Florida, spends about five thousand dollars in a ten-week course to train each student, who pays only for his or her keep. Seasoned clowns do the teaching. Why all the effort and expenditure? Clowns, cross-cultural and worldwide, come with no prejudice, no preconceived idea about the way one ought to think and live. Distrust and credibility gaps are unknown in their milieu. Clowns make an unfriendly world into a friendly one, and the emotional release in those who watch cannot be calculated.

Today, clowns perform in churches (*Time,* September 1, 1980) and hospitals, as well as at the circus. They make people laugh on street corners and in rest homes. Who can know whether or not any researcher will ever document the full range of therapeutic effects? But we do know that a harlequin's face reads like a humor book, and that pantomime (clowns are not permitted to talk) tickles our funny bones. These jovial pranksters, perhaps above all other comedians, have the ability to divert attention.

P. T. Barnum knew instinctively that clowns make up the heart of the circus. In 1871, when Barnum and two partners started the troupe now known as the Ringling Brothers and Barnum and Bailey Circus, clowns learned by on-the-job training. The present owner, Irvin Feld, established the Clown College in 1968 to give more formal shape to the education of aspiring buffoons. Schoolwork begins in the fall, while the circus makes preparation for a new season. About sixty students enroll. They must master juggling, gymnastics, stilts, makeup, costume creation. No one under seventeen years of age may enter the program.

One young clown testifies, "When I see somebody laughing at me, I love it. It feels really good." Some have gone so far as to compare Christ and clowns. Jesus could be trusted, and he could make people laugh (see Elton Trueblood's *The Humor of Christ*, 1964). "I came," said our Lord, "that they may have life, and have it abundantly" (John 10:10b).

Sources of Joy and Laughter

Keep company with the more cheerful sort
of the godly; there is no mirth like the mirth
of believers.

—Richard Baxter

1

The Resurrection Connection

Ecclesiastes 3:4 tells us there is a "time to weep, and a time to laugh; a time to mourn, and a time to dance." The sequence is significant. There is winter before spring, grief prior to joy, death before resurrection.

In the early history of the Greek Orthodox Church, an interesting custom developed. The day after Easter, both ministers and laymen went to church to tell funny stories! Yes, jokes and tales of hilarity. These ancient people had their reason. They must celebrate the enormous prank God played on the devil—Jesus rose victorious over the grave!

This almost overpowering feeling of relief characterizes all true Christians. Stanley Jones used to say he didn't grieve over the awful events in life very long, simply because he knew how it would all turn out. The resurrection documents that God, not evil, is in charge of life.

Why, then, are so many church members Good-Friday Christians? One wonders if certain influential fathers of the church, like Chrysostom, set in motion a chain reaction. Chrysostom, great preacher though he was, actually did a sermon opposing laughter. Preaching at the end of the fourth century, he saw jollity as pagan. He declared that Christians must weep for their sins, that God doesn't want his children to play, and that if the devil can get people engaged in frivolity, he's won the day.

Actually, many leading preachers through the centuries have embraced that very position. But it's wrong, for it rests on premises far from the joy characteristic of the early followers of Christ. In fact, if Christianity had begun under the aegis of Chrysostom's thought, it would have died a natural death. For, you see, the indisputable fact of the resurrection accounts for the church, its persistence, and its radiant witness.

2

That Grand Parenthesis

Beginnings and endings in Scripture are instructive. The first words of Genesis, "In the beginning God . . ." come across with as much positivity as the "grace of the Lord Jesus" benediction closing the Book of Revelation. The Acts of the Apostles commences with Jesus' life and work and terminates with the liberating word *unhindered*. The story of our Lord in the Gospels begins with a marriage feast and concludes with his resurrection.

A great deal in between beginnings and endings, however, relates to sin and the horrors of evil. The Book of Psalms, for example, faces man's bent toward iniquity. Yet notice the first and last clauses of the Book of Psalms: "Blessed is the man . . ." and "Praise the LORD!" This does not imply a facile evaluation of life, for the full scope of human emotions and behaviors finds expression in the body of the psalter. But to read through all hundred and fifty psalms over and again yields the clear finding that the dominant expression is praise.

This framework of joy characterizes those who identify with the Judeo-Christian tradition. Jesus could eat and drink with publicans and sinners because he lived above the meanness of the world. He lived beyond it, enjoying life to the full, and therefore possessed the clear perspective necessary for helping publicans and sinners.

Professor Conrad Hyers, of Gustavus Adolphus College in Minnesota, talks about the "grand parenthesis" in which Jesus did his work. The feast at Cana begins his ministry; the festivals of Easter and Pentecost bring it to a close. He never hid from pain and the cross, from the renunciation and abandonment he suffered (even by his family). But the Lord knew his origin! He knew his destiny! This explains his unrelenting talk about abundant life, hope, faith, cheer, and a hundred more positives.

Jesus' followers know their beginnings, their creation in God; they keep going by the inspired vision of their debarkation point. And that explains the joy of Christ's disciples. No wonder Elton Trueblood could say over dinner with friends, "Isn't it fun to be a Christian!"

3

Freedom to Laugh

The apostle Paul tells us that salvation comes through faith, not law. Law imprisons; grace frees. The Christian's laugh may well express a deeply settled sense of inner freedom.

Herein lies a Christian truth that has its spin-offs in today's society. For example, jails in Missouri recently discovered cartoons as an instrument of prisoner rehabilitation. Humor, it was discovered, opens windows on defining and solving personal problems. Another example: the Ethel Percy Andrus Gerontology Center in Los Angeles developed a humor handbook. It includes comedy-tape lists, funny movies, limericks, bibliography, cartoons—anything to unbind the spirit of the confined.

Peter Berger, insightful writer of our day, declares, "The comic reflects the imprisonment of the human spirit in the world." Humor points to transcendence, to emancipation. Just try to bottle up human beings, especially Christians who know their freedom in Christ!

We all suffer temptation to succumb to negatives—pettiness, for example. But humor is a great antidote, emancipating us to live above the trivial. Often pettiness comes garbed in pomposity and bombast, but God's gift of humor documents our ability to make pretense transparent. And jocularity also helps us see our own pretentious behavior—isn't that part of the genius of laughing at ourselves?

A true theology of play tells us not to take ourselves and circumstances too seriously. Kierkegaard said we should connect with the relative relatively, and relate to the Absolute absolutely. Released laughter and wholesome play restore vision and give us the freedom to distinguish between the relative and the Absolute and to shape thought and behavior accordingly.

The Christian knows the source of laughter: Rock-of-Gibraltar faith. After all, God is bigger than the details of our lives and the problems that threaten to plague us. The more one believes in the sovereignty of God, the greater the freedom to enjoy God's world and even to laugh at life's contradictions.

Paul said, "I . . . died to the law" (Gal. 2:19). Honest-to-goodness freedom is reason enough to have a good laugh. Who can stop the flow of mirth from an unshackled spirit?

4

The God of Surprises

Surprise often triggers laughter. Surprise comes from God himself. We delight in the unexpected.

The grandest of all purely human surprises is the knowledge of sins forgiven. God even forgets our sins, promising never to remember them. He assures us that though our sins are "like scarlet, they shall be as white as snow; though they are red like crimson, they shall become like wool" (Isa. 1:18).

Concert singer David Baker publicly gives his testimony of conversion. He had lived with drugs and in deep sin. Then, one day, an old college classmate began working with David and led him to Christ. Says Dave, "The joy! The sheer joy and reality of Christ! I just can't get over it all." The delight of his words matches the smile on his face—like a child seeing lighted candles on a birthday cake.

The sense of release that comes with forgiveness is enormous. But God's surprises don't stop there. Right through life he delights us with the unexpected, sometimes by his special Presence. Sunday night, sitting in church, I listened to the testimony of a mother who praised God, through tears, because her children were in the kingdom. God came to me in that moment. I smiled. One always does when God comes like that.

Seminarians—nearly all of them—live with money problems. But they cannot resist smiling, even laughing,

41

when they rehearse God's need-meeting provisions. One fellow finds money from an anonymous donor under the door to his dormitory room; another locates a job; still one more hears from his home church. The element of surprise is always there.

The very nature of a joke is tension followed by release. Begin to listen to a story and your muscles actually tighten. Tensity accelerates in anticipation of the anecdote's funny ending. A giggle or two documents your anticipation before the climax. Finally comes the guffaw, fulfillment of your internal wishes to hear something genuinely comical. Hope is vindicated with the surprising close to the story.

Unlike a "funny" story that doesn't quite come off, Christians foresee life's culmination in authentic hope. Hope centers in God, unmovable and sure. The hope in God holds surprises we cannot yet know.

5

Deliverance

Isaiah, in a moment of jubilant inspiration, prophesied like this: "Seek the LORD while he may be found, call upon him while he is near; let the wicked forsake his way, and the unrighteous man his thoughts; let him return to the LORD, that he may have mercy on him, and to our God, for he will abundantly pardon" (Isa. 55:6–7). For Basilea Schfounder of the Sisters of Mary in Darmstadt, Germany, the secret of the joy-saturated life is repentance.

Mother Basilea wrote to a friend that we praise God for many things, "but no exultation on earth can or will surpass the exultation over God's gift of the forgiveness of sins." The psalmist's song—'Bless the Lord, O my soul'—"resounds not only here on earth," she concludes, "but throughout the heavenly spheres, for there is joy in heaven over one sinner who repents."

Christians know the experience of deliverance. Not only in pardon for sin, but also from illness, circumstances, rejection. Whenever deliverance comes, and for whatever reason, always there is that deep relief that brings joy to the heart and laughter from the soul. So a criminal writes that though he is in jail, he is nonetheless "a free man in Christ Jesus. . . ." Someone else says, "For the past two weeks I felt as if the corners of my mouth had been permanently tied down so I couldn't laugh or smile and I wondered why." The heaviness deep in this woman's soul yielded to deliverance. Then she said, "I can smile now and I feel it inside and out. . . ."

The *Book of Common Prayer* gathers up, in its 1662 edition, the experience of joy and comfort that comes with the sense of rescue. Note the vivid figures of those in trouble, then the subsequent relief:

> They reel to and fro, and stagger like a drunken man: and are at their wit's end.
>
> So when they cry unto the LORD in their trouble: he delivereth them out of their distress.
>
> For he maketh the storm to cease: so that the waves thereof are still.
>
> Then are they glad, because they are at rest: and so he bringeth them unto the heaven where they would be.

6
The Spirit
of Christ

Jesus said, "The thief comes only to steal and kill and destroy; I came that they may have life, and have it abundantly" (John 10:10). Samuel Logan Brengle, who became perhaps the most remarkable Salvation Army evangelist America produced, testifies to a profound experience of the Spirit of Christ. He had been seeking the deep things of God for some time. One morning, during this searching period, he awakened "hungering and thirsting just to live this life of fellowship with God," he confesses. Getting up at six o'clock, he opened his Bible and read words from Jesus. "And He gave me such a blessing as I never dreamed a man could have this side of heaven." Brengle tries to describe his joy: "It was an unutterable revelation. It was a heaven of love."

Up and dressed, ready to meet the new day, he walked across Boston Common before breakfast, "weeping for joy and praising God. Oh, how I loved! In that hour I knew Jesus, and I loved Him till it seemed my heart would break with love. I was filled with love for all His creatures," he continues touchingly. "I heard the little sparrows chattering; I loved them. . . . I loved the dogs, I loved the horses, I loved the little urchins on the street, I loved the strangers who hurried past me, I loved the heathen—I loved the whole world!"

One is reminded of Saint Francis of Assisi who, after he had given his inheritance to God, experienced inexpressible joy. Not everyone, of course, has such ecstatic experience of God's grace. Nor does any Christian, Saint Francis and Samuel Logan Brengle included, live on top of the world at all times. After all, the Christian does live by faith in the struggle of life and in that way builds spiritual muscle.

But this one thing is true: resurrection Christians live in the joy of the Lord. Why? Because the spirit of the resurrected Lord lives in his people.

7

Hope

Saint Paul gives us another gem of a statement in Romans 15:13: "May the God of hope fill you with all joy and peace in believing, so that by the power of the Holy Spirit you may abound in hope." On a picture calendar, Canon Bryan Green gives meaningful commentary on Paul's verse. "Joy is the fruit of the Holy Spirit," the distinguished Englishman begins. He goes on to make clear that this happiness is not superficial, not something to keep us forever free from sadness and suffering. Rather, it is inner confidence in God's love and holding power, which "gives a consistent flow of joy deep beneath the waves of trouble and the winds of sorrow. This accounts for the "deep confidence that I am God's forgiven and accepted child and that He will never, never let me go."

Have you ever noticed how hope and joy go together in Scripture?

Paul says that "we rejoice in our hope of sharing the glory of God" (Rom. 5:2).

Isaiah, the prophet of hope, cries, "For you shall go out in joy, and be led forth in peace; the mountains and the hills before you shall break forth into singing, and all the trees of the field shall clap their hands" (Isa. 55:12).

The author of Hebrews talks about "looking to Jesus the pioneer and perfecter of our faith, who for the joy that was set before him endured the cross, despising the shame, and is seated at the right hand of the throne of God" (Heb. 12:2).

Someone rightly observed that "other men see only a hopeless end, but the Christian rejoices in an endless hope." That is why Sam Shoemaker could say, "The surest mark of a Christian is not faith, or even love, but joy." Hope invades mind and heart with joy. That is a law of the human spirit.

Power to Cope

Do not be grieved, for the joy of the LORD is
your strength.

—Nehemiah 8:10

1

Energy

In an historic moment when God's people were tempted to embrace regret, Nehemiah counseled, ". . . do not be grieved, for the joy of the LORD is your strength" (Neh. 8:10). The people obeyed and had a party! In that festive mood they made "great rejoicing" (v. 12).

Sorrow depletes energies; joy replaces them. Restoration starts in the brain, moves to the nervous system, and finally encompasses the whole body. Both the chemical and electrical functions of brain and body get into the act. Laughter kicks the endocrine system into motion. The hormones secreted give "runner's high."

Have you noticed how alert you feel, how vigorous, after a good laugh? You sense the same after brisk and sprightly exercise, like running or swimming.

The hormones, called catecholamines, move into the blood system, and the enhanced circulation generates more laughter and encourages bodily well-being. The pituitary gland functions, and that may be responsible for activating endorphins and enkephalins, the body's natural painkillers.

That's not all. The brain's right side increases in chemical activity, important because the right hemisphere controls emotions and creativity. Actually, both right and left sides of the brain work together in exceptional harmony when we enter into a happy mood.

Moreover, a good laugh does something to the fibers of the

nervous system. Initiating charges in the brain, laughter generates both electrical and chemical impulses related to the hypothalamus, the message-control center. Messages go to the cerebral cortex, the place where discernment is activated. Is it any wonder that hard, cognitive problems yield to the fresh energy now in the brain?

Here is a law of wholesome life: play, fun, and laughter feed the entire system, mental and physical, to heighten energy for productivity and efficiency.

2

A Weapon

Observe the subtle wisdom of Job 3:25: "For the thing that I fear comes upon me, and what I dread befalls me." This well-taken warning relates to life the way it happens, for negative thoughts give birth to negative ordeals, but positive thoughts yield positive experiences.

Humor is God's weapon against worries and the eventualities they inspire. A highjacker once commanded passengers not to make a move; he had a gun. He entered the pilot's area, but a professional comedian got everyone laughing in the highjacker's absence. And when he came back and saw all the people overtly laughing, he concluded they did not take him seriously, lost his nerve, and gave up!

Herman Jose, a Portuguese TV comedian from Lisbon, has great fun with political leaders, but he only aims at those who themselves see the funny side of life. "Reagan tells jokes," he comments, but goes on to say, "I leave the communists alone because they have no sense of humor." Herman knows that laughing people survive and go on to victories; he also knows that those who cannot or will not laugh have already mapped out their doom.

A doctor said of a friend, "He will never have a breakdown because he has a hair-trigger laugh." Likewise, an insightful leader said of a colleague going through the stress of adjusting to retirement, "He laughs easily, so I know he will come through this period okay."

Humor documents one's contact with reality. A grip on the facts means mental health, which signifies wholeness.

One of the most interesting experiments in laughter research relates to alcoholism. The South African Brain Research Institute now uses in therapy not conventional heavy sedation, but laughing gas, oxygen and nitrous oxide. After treating about seven hundred cases in the new way, they note the reversal of both physical and psychological withdrawal symptoms and also the shortening of detoxification periods. The success rate is so high that some with expertise in the field of rehabilitation believe the new treatment will become standard.

We now know body chemistry alters with laughter. It can change our whole psychology. Then, clearly, it is a weapon against, and a way of coping with, anxiety and negativities of all sorts.

3

A Way of Seeing

Humorists are winners. They win because they can see clearly.

A certain novelist probably determined the success of his career because he used laughter as an agent for keeping his sight at 20/20. This is the way it happened. As a beginning reporter for a small newspaper, he got a letter from his father, who wrote impatiently about his son never amounting to a row of beans. Though annoyed, the young reporter wrote not a blistering reply, but indicated that though at twenty-one he seemed incapable, yet he had in fact thought out his life goals. His plan for achievement? At thirty he intended to be a great newspaper reporter; at forty a great editor; at fifty a great story writer; at sixty a great fiction writer; at seventy a great grandfather; at eighty a great admirer of beautiful women; at ninety a great loss to the community.

His father had a good laugh. And, significantly, the years saw the son's career proceed along the very lines he predicted in that amusing letter.

I have a friend who refuses to worry, for he knows anxiety fogs his lenses and makes focusing impossible. Although my friend fought big problems for forty years, he insisted on dissipating his fret potential in humor. Riotously funny, he keeps his problems reduced to a size easily seen and puts them in a corner where he can keep a bead on them. He never allows them to tower over him so they can look down from some mocking position. Moreover, humor becomes a pair of spectacles through which he sees life whole. This way of seeing held him to faith and kept him collected through the long illness of his wife and, finally, successful surgery for her. Now she enjoys good health, and together they relish retirement in Christian service both overseas and at home.

Says Irving Oyle, a medical doctor, "Positive, beautiful thoughts trigger the release of beneficial hormones in the body and these in turn help the body to heal itself." But, he says, "If you presume that you live in a hostile universe, the reaction to that presumption is what wears out your body." Dr. Oyle concludes, "Faith creates the hormones that make you live longer."

And what generates faith? Prayer, affirmative thinking, positive achievement, and, of course, humor. How do you look at your world? If through hostile, paranoid eyes, you can change your prescription. Let God be your ophthalmologist.

4

Rising
to Challenges

Abraham Lincoln, given a great and godly vision for America, suffered as many failures as any person in our history. He tried farming, and failed; he attempted to make a living by commercial water transport, and failed; he made an effort at teaching school, but failed. Even his marriage proved tragic. He ran for public office time and again, failing more often than not. And when at last he won the presidency, he inherited a war.

Any ordinary person would have thrown in the sponge. Not Lincoln. Humor and a fine mind kept him alive and thinking clearly. During the nonstop disasters of the Civil War, this lanky, towering human being walked the midnight corridors of the White House in his red flannel nightwear, hoping to find someone still awake, someone with whom he could share a funny tale from his reading. Reporters tell us he had a laugh like the neigh of a wild horse, a laugh that became famous for its hearty and full-bodied character.

In a tense board meeting, the wise executive will not beat his head against a stone wall but will create an opening in the atmosphere with wit and humor. A funny story or pleasant aside will come as welcome relief, clear minds, and forward problem solving.

Much the same psychology obtains when we watch a thriller on TV. The commercials come every fourteen minutes or so, but they do more than advertise: they bring comic relief. They say, "All's normal, after all," a message necessary for the restoration of perspective.

Moreover, wholesome laughter indicates that the one doing the laughing enjoys self-respect and healthy faith. It says of a leader, especially one going through the throes of defeating the odds against him, that he can, after all, do his job. Laughter says you believe in yourself, and that helps others believe in you.

Let laughter reign when it comes. It is oil for the engines that rise to challenges and work miracles.

5

Laughing
Toward Old Age

Norman Cousins got plenty of skeptical laughs when he claimed laughter could assist in the healing process. One doctor, for example, in a national magazine penned an article in which he raised some red flags about the Cousins thesis. But while the skeptics laughed, the researchers investigated. Two delightful conclusions from geriatrics studies are these: joy encourages longevity and also contributes to quality of life in the elderly.

Laughter increases respiration, aids oxygen exchange, and heightens muscular activity. It contributes to a better-functioning cardiovascular system, does the same for the sympathetic nervous system, and sets off the body's own pain-lessening enzymes. Beta-endorphins come into production, and some believe they create that good feeling we all have when we laugh wholeheartedly.

Like physical exercise, laughter reduces depression, stress, and hypertension, all key challenges for most human beings, especially older people. With emotional and physical therapy comes the potential for minimizing the possibility of strokes and heart attacks, ulcers, chronic headaches, and a host of other ailments.

Dr. Jeffrey Goldstein, a psychologist from Temple University in Philadelphia, says right out there is a definite possibility that laughter relates "in several ways to longevity." That news is getting around, and it is therefore no surprise that the American Association of Retired Persons engaged their members in a project to solicit humor ideas. It started with a letter to the *AARP News Bulletin* written by Ethel Wise of Atlanta. "I am a volunteer trying to bring laughter to residents of nursing homes and patients in hospitals or hospices," she wrote. "I urge your members to send along their suggestions . . . because my people are waiting to laugh." The response surprised, even amazed, her. From every state in the Union, and other areas around the world like Australia and the Virgin Islands, letters came daily. "This enormous response has restored my faith in mankind," she commented.

Cards, tapes, cartoon scrapbooks, magazines, and books all appeared in the mail. Creative suggestions came galore: entertainment from such service clubs as the Lions and Kiwanis; joke scrapbooks for looking at or reading aloud; ideas for getting help from the local public libraries; how to use high school and college groups, and community choirs, too.

People sense that cheer is a good doctor. In fact, Tom Mullen, in *Laughing Out Loud and Other Religious Experiences*, says, "Specialists in gerontology have observed that healthy, very elderly patients invariably demonstrate a spirit of fun."

6

Taking Life in Good Humor

The apostle Paul exhorts us to have no anxiety, not even about little things. George Burns, in *How to Live to Be 100— or More*, teaches us some things about minimizing anxiety. "If you ask me what is the single-most important key to longevity, I would have to say it is avoiding worry, stress, and tension. And if you didn't ask me," old George concludes wryly, "I'd still have to say it."

So he created a book to help us. He outlines his exercise program—the Knee-Hi, the Pedal Pusher, the Neck Stretcher. He has fun with his dietary pattern—prunes come in as a breakfast favorite—but the bottom line is that he eats very little. He helps us avoid negatives by exhorting that if we expect to get to age one hundred, "you've got to have a positive attitude," and: "Even if you're going to fail, be positive about it. That way you'll be a successful failure."

Toward the end of his book, Burns talks about death in a chapter called "Stay Away from Funerals, Especially Yours." George cautions against looking in the obituary column: "If your name isn't there, go ahead and have breakfast." If he himself ever finds his name in the column, "I'd still have breakfast. I'm not leaving on an empty stomach."

Whether or not the famous comedian knows it, he advocates a system of good health under the metaphor of humor. The eminently wholesome attitude he projects much of the time is good for people of any age. As the jacket implies, the book is "a priceless guide to levity and longevity which will have you charging on to 100—and laughing all the way."

7

Comedians
Help Us Cope

The psalmist exhorts us to do away with our fears. "I sought the LORD, and he answered me, and delivered me from all my fears" (Ps. 34:4). Then the poet gives us the clue: "Look to him [the LORD] and be radiant; so your faces shall never be ashamed" (v. 5).

Francis Schaeffer believed that radiant witness lies, at least in part, in what he called the Christian's "beauty." I agree. But the way we lose that glow is to take ourselves and the world too seriously. Cartoonists and comedians use their art to release us from that seriousness; they poke fun at our wrinkled brows and, in so doing, translate wrinkles into smiles.

Will Rogers knew that having fun, say at the government's expense, may do us about as much good as coming up with solutions. "I don't make jokes," he commented with his Oklahoma cowboy wit; "I just watch the government and report what I see."

Bill Cosby's great gift is to help us handle reality—the tensions of daily family life, for example, which he reduces to size. His tone calls up, in each of us, the child within, and children see life through unencumbered eyes and find ways of managing it.

Jack Benny was "the sucker," Jackie Gleason "the helpless one." All comedians work with tragedy, the basic stuff of comedy. When any impossible situation hangs like a specter, humans find relief in a valve called humor. Thus Steve Allen comments, "To look purposely for the element of humor in an uncomfortable situation is to make use of an important procedure in emotional control, in the maintenance of one's own mental health. We sometimes joke and laugh," he concludes, "because we do not wish to fight or destroy ourselves."

Thank God for the humorists in society who serve by robbing us of sadness, a great drain on energies. They prove themselves God's instruments to help us cope with life and restore radiance, the hallmark of vigor and vitality.

Worship and Joy

*When Christian worship is dull and joyless,
Jesus Christ has been left outside—that is the
only possible explanation.*

—James S. Stewart

1

Joy in God's House

Isaiah, prophesying in the name of the Lord, speaks of those who identify with authentic religion. ". . . these I will bring to my holy mountain," says God through his servant, "and make them joyful in my house of prayer . . ." (Isa. 56:7).

On the surface, it would seem that the apostle Paul disagreed with Isaiah, for Paul warns the Ephesians against levity, which he says is "not fitting" (Eph. 5:4). Saint Benedict similarly cautioned monks against laughter, and another monk who lived a long time ago, Peter Damiani, claimed laughter the most difficult of offenses to eradicate.

But Benedict and Damiani suffered an exegetical conditioning that blinded them from seeing writers like Paul in context. Later in that fifth chapter of Ephesians, Paul exhorts worshiping Christians to address "one another in psalms and hymns and spiritual songs, singing and making melody to the Lord with all your heart" (v. 19). Martin Luther evidently read Paul in context, for he declared with a lot of conviction that "it is pleasing to the dear God whenever thou rejoicest or laughest from the bottom of thy heart." And one suspects that this introducer of joyous singing into the Christian church was not averse to laughing out loud during worship services.

Back to Paul and the "levity" he cried out against. We must remember that this levity means boorishness, laughing at the sacred or at something that should be treated with respect. A boor is ill-mannered, uncouth; filth may come from his mouth. By complete contrast we have verse 20 of chapter 5, where the apostle identifies the object of our rejoicing: the Lord Jesus Christ. And just there, or rather, just in *him,* we find the source of our delight: the resurrected Christ, victorious over all evil. James S. Stewart rightly declares, "When Christian worship is dull and joyless, Jesus Christ has been left outside—that is the only possible explanation."

But actual laughter? Is there a place for that in Christian worship? Yes. Laughter is a recognition of our finitude in contrast to our ultimate security in Christ. Reinhold Niebuhr says humor is a "prelude to faith," that laughter is "the beginning of prayer" and "a vestibule to the temple of confession." The purpose of worship is the renewal that comes with submission to the One mightier than ourselves. To catch a glimpse of the omnipotent God in contrast to our limitations may well bring a relieved smile to our lips.

And our security? That comes when we find our confidence in the God that was and is in Christ. Gordon W. Allport, the Harvard psychologist, makes the astute suggestion that "A case might be made for the potentially superior humor of the religious person who has settled once and for all what things are of ultimate value, sacred and untouchable. For then nothing else in the world need be taken seriously." In Christ, matters of ultimate value are indeed settled.

2

Clowns Go
to Church

Buried deep in the heart of every person is the necessity for festivity; that relates to why we often refer to worship as "celebration." The Bible talks a great deal about feasts and festivals, especially high sacred occasions. Notice that feasts are "to the Lord" (Exod. 5:1; 12:14; etc.).

Festive expression in our day has taken what at first seems a strange turn. The Reverend Floyd Shaffer, a Lutheran minister, sometimes dresses as a clown. He will, for example, preside over Holy Communion services attended by nearly two hundred clowns. No, he is not sacrilegious; but he is entirely serious about celebration.

Actually dozens of ministers in very recent years have engaged in clowning as a vehicle for Christian communication. They call themselves "fools for Christ's sake," since God "made foolish the wisdom of the world" (1 Cor. 1:20). Christ and the clown have much in common, say these pastors. Christ was childlike, simple, enjoyed the everyday things of life, believed in everyone's potential. And Jesus did indeed see possibilities in everybody, even so-called hopeless cases.

The clown is a metaphor for transcending limits. Jesus healed people, was even resurrected from the dead. A clown does "impossible" things—makes water squirt out of a boutonniere, rides a bicycle across a tightrope. Christ can take problem people and transform them, as he did the rugged

Peter who became the first preacher of the Christian church and won thousands to the gospel.

Hundreds of years ago the church expected clowns in worship services. They popped up from the congregation and mimed, did magic, mocked evil, performed in any of the ways clowns do, but in the interests of illustrating gospel truth to an illiterate age. The clowns' make-believe disarmed people and somehow opened the doors to belief. That's why some street preachers and church evangelists dress and perform as clowns today.

Clowns, moreover, help us laugh at our helplessness. And once we laugh at it, we have admitted our need. Admitting is the price of admission into the kingdom. Jesus told us that when we become as little children we enter the kingdom of God. Buffoons have a way of clobbering artificiality, that ever-threatening blockade to God.

Well, no one wants mere entertainment in church. But we can thank God for several thousand clown ministry groups active in our time, for they remind us that letting down our barriers, so that God can come into our hearts, is a joyous and liberating affair.

3

Worship and the Right Side of the Brain

In a moment of inspired worship, Isaiah sings, "I will greatly rejoice in the LORD, my soul shall exult in my God; for he has clothed me with the garments of salvation, he has covered me with the robe of righteousness, as a bridegroom decks himself with a garland, and as a bride adorns herself with her jewels" (Isa. 61:10). The joyous and pictorial quality of these words represents perfectly the dramatic nature of worship as the Bible understands it.

Worship is essentially a right-brained activity—imaginative, picture producing, poetic, musical. The left brain is rational and cognitive. The right brain is emotional and warm, the left hemisphere calculating and analytical.

We are not surprised, then, when we learn that the laughter locus resides in the right brain. Research into victims who suffered right-hemispherical brain damage showed them incapable of laughing at stories normal people found hilarious. While the left brain relates to some kinds of humor, the right brain often initiates laughter responses.

Serious material tends to be left-brained, and it communicates with corresponding difficulty. When, in fact, we need to say something heavy, especially in an audience made up of people with mixed intellectual orientations, the best way to get through is first to do or say something imaginative. To get the emotions moving is to pave the runway into the left brain.

The Christian church has always intuited this principle. Thus Holy Communion re-enacts the Last Supper; baptism re-lives the baptism of our Lord; good sermons deliver imaginatively. Temple University studies revealed that only 7 percent of our communication is verbal; 38 percent is tonal; and 55 percent is nonverbal body language.

Wise worship leaders know that to get through to the people they must resist cold abstraction, modify the linear, and process the logical. The painter's palette, the dramatist's movement, the humorist's stories, must have their appropriate place. Although neither preachers nor parishioners need be frivolous, every human being craves genuine communication. That ministry comes naturally and fulfillingly when we sing in the spirit of *Old Hundredth:* "Him serve with mirth, His praise forthtell."

4

How Did We Get So Sober?

The writer to the Hebrews, speaking of Jesus, talks about the "joy that was set before him"—that's why the Lord could endure the cross, despising its shame (Heb. 12:2). But the cross seems to have taken precedence over the joy. Historically, Jesus has become the man of sorrows, acquainted with grief, more than the Son of God filled with the joy of his Father.

Yet the mystery is this: the Bible, in both the Old and New Testaments, carries from beginning to end, from Genesis to Revelation, a note of exuberance. Words for "joy" occur some 125 times in the Gospels alone!

Renan, the French writer, says Jesus "traversed Galilee in the midst of a continual feast. . . . His entering a house was considered a joy and a blessing. He stopped in the villages and the large farms, where he received an eager hospitality. . . . The mothers. . .brought him their children in order that he might touch them. Women came to pour oil upon his head, and perfume on his feet."

The reason we have been misled goes back to Plato and Aristotle. These Greek minds examined tragedy and comedy and concluded that the human race comes across more honorably when seen through the eyes of tragic-drama rather than through the eyes of comic-drama. Comedy sees humanity less than it is; tragedy perceives it nobler than it is.

So, when the theologians tackled Bible interpretation, they took Greek cues with them. They constructed a dark framework within which to work—man's depravity, the evilness of the world, and the answer in the crucifixion. The shove from Greek thinkers persists to this day: the chief theologian of the twentieth century, Karl Barth, devotes but a single page to humor out of all the pages in his multivolume *Dogmatics*. True, he discusses the resurrection, salvation, and a good many components of the Good News. Nonetheless, the little space given to humor symbolizes his tendency to look at the serious side of life before the lighter, upbeat dimensions.

Happy emotions, theologians and ministers have come to believe, are unworthy. Ambrose of Milan informed his clergy that "joking should be avoided even in small talk, so that some more serious topic is not made light of. . . ."

But many people have avoided the church because they get the message that only depressives, at least terribly austere people, can really be good Christians!

5

Preaching
and Scripture

No one can read Isaiah's famous words about the preacher without catching the prophet's own bounteous zest: "How beautiful upon the mountains are the feet of him who brings good tidings, who publishes peace, who brings good tidings of good, who publishes salvation, who says to Zion, 'Your God reigns'" (Isa. 52:7). Nothing doleful there!

Nor in the Scriptures as a whole, does the mournful out-run the joyful in the story of either the Hebrew nation or the beginnings of the Christian community. God laughs (Ps. 2:4); God plays (Job 41:5); God likes us to laugh (Ps. 126), and God promises laughter to his own (Luke 6:21b). Together these texts make a beautiful collage:

He who sits in the heavens laughs. . . .

Will you play with him as with a bird. . . .?

Then our mouth was filled with laughter, and our tongue with shouts of joy. . . .

Blessed are you that weep now, for you shall laugh.

The Scriptures include games and playing, fables, and plays on words (some passages yield their deepest meaning only when the wordplay comes to light). Jesus' words include irony; some Old Testament passages project satire. We have a whole set of books called Wisdom Literature, which includes wit and riddlelike material. And no one can read the Book of Proverbs without smiling sooner or later.

In our day we are blessed with a growing number of preachers who have picked up on the joyful note in Scripture. They are unafraid to have fun and to engage their listeners in a good laugh. Lee F. Tuttle, in *Profiles of 20th Century Pulpit Giants*, treats twenty-four preachers and finds characteristics common to all, "but perhaps a sense of humor was the most unanimously a major [feature]." The reason is clear: these pulpit giants know who is in charge of the world, that God will win out in the end, that acceptance of our finitude brings release, and that supposing we are little gods only makes us terribly ridiculous. They know that revolutionaries cannot laugh, but that liberators find delight everywhere they turn, that serious religion must be balanced by the lighter side of life.

Leighton Ford, himself a happy preacher, has had lots of fun over his relationship to Billy Graham, his brother-in-law. He has been called Graham's son-in-law, even mother-in-law and sister-in-law. Presenting Leighton Ford to collegians in chapel, a presiding educator twisted his tongue to everyone's delight: "We are happy to have Leighton Ford as our speaker this morning," he commenced by way of introduction. "Perhaps some of you don't know that Leighton Ford is married to Billy Graham's brother."

Tittering all around. But the distinguished presenter, unaware of his error and nonplussed by audience response, added, "That makes Leighton Billy Graham's son-in-law."

Now the students could not help but roll in the aisles. The usually careful public speaker, trying desperately to mend whatever must have gone wrong, only fell completely into a comedy of errors by concluding, "So . . . now I present to you, Leighton Ford's brother-in-law, Billy Graham!"

6

Mirth, Balance, and Therapy

Laughter research, in uncovering crucial data for information and improved living, signals mirth's capacity to restore balance to our lives—balance in terms of mental outlook, perspective, physiology, faith, and wholeness. Saint Paul admonishes, "And let the peace of Christ rule in your hearts. . . . and be thankful" (Col. 3:15). In the very next verse, Paul's merry heart surfaces with the further admonition to "sing psalms and hymns and spiritual songs with thankfulness in your hearts to God."

We now know that laughter can reestablish peace, and when that happens our very physiologies change. For example, we have learned that kinetic energies, banked in the body's organs, come to release in laughter, thus giving us motivation, drives, and forward thrust. Moreover, mirth-response testing shows humor to be a factor in restoring and maintaining emotional well-being. Interestingly, the maladjusted persons in one test group reacted negatively to the comic. Nervousness, resentment, and general unhappiness resulted. Contrariwise, normal psyches enjoyed the delights of a funny story or joke, and their anxiety levels lowered accordingly. Historically, psychiatrists have probably looked on humor as an anxiety-reducing instrument.

Worship, private or public, ought to contribute to anxiety reduction. Robert Louis Stevenson, however, did not believe that was always the case; in fact, he sometimes found going to church triggered discouragement.

Worship, by its very nature, is supposed to help us handle the incongruities of life. Reinhold Niebuhr is exactly right when he declares that both faith and humor help us cope with incompatibilities. Faith, Professor Niebuhr believed, deals with ultimate discordances, while humor helps us manage disparities in the here and now.

Bob W. Parrott, in *God's Sense of Humor,* has quite a lot to say about the incongruities of life. He points out that the recognition of them from the pulpit or on one's knees is essential to understanding that God himself is in control. When that knowledge sets in, faith operates. Wholesome humor rescues us from feelings of superiority, the awful soberness that stifles liberation and spawns unbelief.

Do your own research. Notice the sense of contented adjustment that settles on a congregation after a good laugh. Comic relief can do that when people struggle to listen to a sermon, but the relief relates specially to the struggle of life itself. Observe your own feelings in private devotion when you see something in Scripture that tickles your mirth response into action. A happy heart refurbishes the mind with a sharpened view of things. Indeed, sometimes a whole new panorama stretches out before one's mind, bringing the fresh light and renewed strength that signifies balance.

7

Therapeutic Preaching

Surely Jesus had a twinkle in his eye when he referred to the pompous Pharisees who "preach, but do not practice." He denounces hypocrisy in Matthew 23, and the preaching-but-not-practicing bit gets at the center of all he says on the subject. One mark of some great preachers of history is humility that allows them to see themselves for what they are and laugh about it. That attitude is contagious because people identify with imperfection. Only muffled laughs come in the presence of imperfection trying to be perfect.

Who the preacher is, then, becomes more important than what he says. When his authority has no power to rob him of self-awareness, when he can say by his very humor that he, too, is a sinner saved by grace, he plugs in to his audience.

Malcolm Muggeridge believes humor is the "disparity between human aspiration and human performance." The preacher who admits that will sooner or later be both humorous and therapeutic. Not that we can always be funny about the disparity between the ideal and the real; some things are just plain heavy to bear. But after they are dealt with head-on, the therapy needed may be a good laugh. We cannot help but be impressed by Jesus' straightforward handling of the heavies in the story of the prodigal; and after that he wisely injects relief with "Let us make merry."

The spirit of Jesus' preaching is the spirit of the historic public prayer, the *Sursum corda*, "Lift Up Your Hearts," often prayed responsively:

> Lift up your hearts.
> *We lift them up unto the Lord.*
> O Lord, open thou our eyes.
> *That we may behold wondrous things out of thy law.*
> O Lord, open thou our lips.
> *And our mouth shall show forth thy praise.*
> Praise ye the Lord.
> *The Lord's name be praised.*

Gratitude

Gratitude is not only the greatest of virtues, but the parent of all others.

—Cicero

1

The Attitude of Gratitude

The theme song of the Book of Psalms is thanks. For example, Psalm 106:1: "Praise the LORD! O give thanks to the LORD, for he is good; for his steadfast love endures for ever!"

America's first woman poet, Anne Bradstreet (1612–1672), daughter of a Massachusetts Bay Colony governor and also mother of eight, penned the following verse straight from her heart. It is a prayer of thanks, written when her husband returned home safely:

> What shall I render
> to thy Name,
> or how thy Praises speak;
> My thankes
> how shall I testefye?
> O Lord,
> thou know'st I'm weak.
> What could I more desire?
> But Thankfulness,
> even all my dayes,
> I humbly this Require.

Gratitude brings joy, often instantly. The reason for that is a spiritual law articulated by John Wesley: "Praise opens the door to more grace." And awareness of a fresh renewal of God's grace only generates more gratitude, which in turn gives birth to multiplied joy.

2

Gratitude, Health, and Wholeness

Proverbs 16:24 reveals profound wisdom: "Pleasant words are like a honeycomb, sweetness to the soul and health to the body." Gratefulness moves us to happy thoughts and language. That, in turn, as we now know from biochemical studies, stimulates brain and body to physical health.

The reverse also obtains, which is why E. Stanley Jones lists the twelve apostles of ill health:

1. Anger
2. Resentments
3. Fear
4. Worry
5. Desire to dominate
6. Self-preoccupation
7. Guilt
8. Sexual impurity
9. Jealousy
10. A lack of creative activity
11. Inferiorities
12. A lack of love

The magic of a thankful spirit is that it has the power to replace anger with love, resentment with happiness, fear with faith, worry with peace, the desire to dominate with the wish to play on a team, self-preoccupation with concern for the needs of others, guilt with an open door to forgiveness, sexual impurity with honor and respect, jealousy with joy at another's success, lack of creativity with inspired productivity, inferiorities with dignity, a lack of love with an abundance of self-sharing.

Medical and mental-health authorities would agree that the above twelvefold transformation spells both inner and outer well-being. Even for one physically crippled, praise-filled lips bring wholeness and, in addition, uplift to those in the presence of the invalid. Such was the case with Amy Carmichael, who for two decades administered the orphanage in India from her bed! When Billy Graham visited Dohnavur, locale of Miss Carmichael's home for destitute girls, he had to remove himself to the garden, where he could weep in private. To read her life story is to learn of the remarkable consistency of her joyful spirit, whose wellspring was gratitude.

The genius of gratitude, unlike self-sympathy, is in the joy-producing result: wholeness.

3
A Key Clue
to Happiness

"In the world you have tribulation," promises Jesus, and then he gives a higher promise, "but be of good cheer, I have overcome the world" (John 16:33b). The first clause of this statement is simply a recognition of reality—life does have its battles. The last portion of the verse is admonition to joyful gratitude, source of happiness. "How happy a person is," John Miller observed, "depends upon the depth of his gratitude."

But it is naive to believe that recognition of God's goodness is something one turns on or off like a water tap. A grateful attitude is, as someone wisely observed, "both delicate and mysterious. It can be crushed by the uplifting of a skeptical eyebrow; yet its psychology is hidden in the divine love." Are we left, then, to the whim of circumstance? No indeed. The whole quest for a thankful heart, with its inevitable issuance in happiness, relates to developing a mind-set strong as an army with banners, sturdy as the Rock of Gibraltar. We are called to establish gratitude as a lifestyle.

How do we establish that lifestyle? Three suggestions help answer that fundamental question:

1. Ask for a grateful heart; ask simply and sincerely:

> O Lord, that lends me life,
> Lend me a heart replete with thankfulness!
> —William Shakespeare

2. Surrender your ego. Mark Twain got at this in his own ironical way: "If you pick up a starving dog and make him prosperous, he will not bite you; that is the principal difference between a dog and a man." Receiving gratefully requires humility; the practice of such selflessness develops strong spirituality.

3. Decide to be grateful, whether you feel like it or not. The old James-Lange theory of psychology, that we feel like doing things after we start doing them, has a lot of merit. While that doesn't always work, it functions better than 90 percent of the time. So, say you are grateful, whether you want to or not, and you will usually feel grateful—and happier because of your willing expression of thanks.

4

Remembering
with Gratitude

The word *remember,* in both Old and New Testaments, appears often and always with significant meaning. Psalm 98, for example, exclaims, "O sing to the LORD a new song, for he has done marvelous things! His right hand and his holy arm have gotten him victory."

What basically strikes the Bible reader is the praise posture of the writers, the framework of gratefulness that holds the picture of the past. Even when things had gone badly for the Israelites or Christians, the thrust of optimism was there. Not that the Scripture avoids the realities of the past; escapism never issues in joy and is never the stance of the Bible writers.

What we have in Holy Writ is the unveiling of a secret to handling memories, personal and social. The secret is this: gratitude makes it possible not only to live with the past but to see it in a meaningful light. We can live with anything so long as we know there is purpose to it. Nor must we have all the details in mind; even when we cannot sense everything, we live in the faith that God uses all. Romans 8:28 promises that all things work together for good to those who love God. That is a law of life. God wastes nothing; he creates out of the chaotic, re-creates out of the discarded, and often puts things back better than they were before, as in the case of Job.

Individuals who have experienced healing for bad memories find that when gratitude reigns, the past is put into perspective and peace follows. The process of becoming self-aware and openly honest may be painful catharsis. But it *is* catharsis. Anger turns to constructive uses; love takes over the will; hope replaces hate. Gratitude is the dynamic that makes therapy reality. Cicero had it right: "Gratitude is not only the greatest of virtues, but the parent of all the others."

We must take the initiative in gratitude. Said Charles E. Jefferson, the American preacher, "Gratitude is born in hearts that take time to count up past mercies." That may not be as difficult as it first appears, for psychologists have discovered that we tend to remember good experiences and forget the bad. So, when we suffer some little injustice, we had best laugh it off and let it rest in God's kind hand, knowing he works for our good. That is a sure way to live in joy instead of bitterness, and it is the real documentation for memory healing.

5

Giving Thanks Always

The Book of Philippians is filled with the admonition to give thanks in all things.

Bill Stidger, that unusual preacher and teacher of preachers, sat about with friends one Thanksgiving Day during the Great Depression. The grumbling that emerged finally prompted someone to suggest a change of conversation to something more positive. After all, Christians should express affirmation and appreciation! And how about starting with those who had done them good?

Bill thought of Mrs. Wendt, the high-school teacher who had introduced him to Tennyson, Browning, and other poets. The upshot: he took pen in hand and wrote Mrs. Wendt a thank-you note. The response he got from the lady, now very old and in a rest home, was so gratifying that he began to send appreciation letters to other folk. In fact, he determined to make November his annual write-thank-you-notes month.

He remembered, for example, how Mrs. McDowell, wife of Bishop William F. McDowell, had been kind to him before a speaking engagement. "Seeing that I was tired out," remembers Bill Stidger, "Mrs. McDowell put me to bed to rest, and I was so grateful for that motherly thoughtfulness that I never forgot it." Yet, he admitted he had never once said thank-you. But by the time he got around to sending a letter,

Mrs. McDowell had died. So he wrote the bishop, rehearsing the memory in some detail. Dr. Stidger received a most touching response in which Bishop McDowell confessed that tears came to his eyes. He explained that he called out his wife's name and started to show her the letter—he had forgotten for the moment that she was gone. "Will," as the bishop called his younger friend, would never know how the letter "has warmed my spirit. I have been walking in the glow of it all day long."

As it turned out, that letter was typical of over five hundred responses Professor Stidger got over a ten-year period.

The apostle Paul told us to give thanks in any and all circumstances, even to take the initiative in expressing gratitude. I, for one, want to be like Paul and Bill Stidger. God, grant me the grace of expressed gratitude.

6

The Prayer
That Brings Joy

In the crucible of his suffering, Paul cried out from his prison cell with words that would make one think he wrote from a comfortable hotel room overlooking the Tiber River. He announced, "Have no anxiety about anything, but in everything by prayer and supplication with thanksgiving let your requests be made known to God" (Phil. 4:6). As if that were not enough joyful expression, he added, "And the peace of God, which passes all understanding, will keep your hearts and your minds in Christ Jesus" (v. 7).

"A single grateful thought toward heaven," said a sensitive soul, "is the most complete prayer." There's something about gratitude that opens God's heart and lets answers to prayer flow freely. Perhaps God's feelings are rather like ours; after all, we feel good and generous when someone expresses genuine appreciation to us. If "gratitude is the homage of the heart, rendered to God for his goodness," as Nathaniel Parker Willis said, then God's heart and soul are touched by it, and he unleashes heaven's blessings in a great Niagara of returning love.

In my work as a minister and counselor, I have noticed that those who make thankfulness the style of their lives get answers to their prayers—even answers hard to come by. I have also observed the reverse: those who complain miss the answers God desires to give, and their problems multiply.

Charles Spurgeon, a long time ago, put this truth in succinct language: "When we bless God for mercies we prolong them. When we bless Him for miseries we usually end them."

One other facet of this divine reality is that we help God with His work when we share the best. That is why Edwin Percy Whipple observed, "God is glorified, not by our groans, but by our thanksgivings." An American preacher, instructing other American preachers, warned that it is a sin to send people away from church on flat tires. By the same token, it is wrong for any Christian to spread negativity. But it is as right as rain to circulate God's Good News. Then others, too, will have the door opened to the answered prayer that brings joy.

7

The Witness of Gratitude

Paul, closing Philippians, says an astonishing thing: "All the saints greet you, especially those of Caesar's household" (Phil. 4:22). Imagine! Saints in Caesar's household.

Now, how in the world did Paul succeed in getting converts in this tightly closed pagan in-group? Surely the texture and context of the whole Book of Philippians gives us the answer. Throughout the letter, Paul praises God. Even when he has hard things to say, he couches them in a thankful tone. The poor man had every reason to complain, but he did not. In point of fact, the student of the letter to the Philippian church will search in vain even to discover where Paul was imprisoned. Was it Rome? Was it Caesarea? Or Ephesus? Scholars suggest all three places, but we cannot know for sure.

Gratitude like that makes people ask probing questions. What causes such a lifestyle? Where does it come from? What sustains the suffering man's joy? No doubt Paul heard questions like these from Caesar's servants. And surely he had ready answers. When, at last, the emperor's workers saw the transparent faith of their prisoner, realized he was not faking, they wanted the same power in their own lives. With that opening into their hearts, Paul led them to Christ.

The evangelism of the world is our biggest calling. Our next largest challenge is to create the evangelists to do the job. The first mark, the most telling characteristic required, is the attitude of gratitude. Read the first church-history account, the Acts of the Apostles, and try to come to a definition of Christian witness. After study and thought you will suggest such words as "radiance," "contagion," "joy." To this day that is what brings people to the feet of Christ. And that is what keeps people coming in a steady flow to the gospel. We noticed in an earlier reading segment that the final word of the Acts of the Apostles is "unhindered." Nothing stops the witness of glad gratitude.

Faith and the Joyous Spirit

My most cherished possession I wish I could leave you is my faith in Jesus Christ, for with him and nothing else you can be happy, but without him and with all else you'll never be happy.

—Patrick Henry

1

The Joyous Liberation
of Faith

Jesus declared, "You will know the truth, and the truth will make you free" (John 8:32). Faith and humor live close to one another; they throw up the blinds of the soul to see truth, which makes us free and joyous. Truth is our homeland, the soul's native soil. We are made for truth; it is our natural place of residence.

Authentic faith lifts restraints—it lets us out of the jail we erect for ourselves and breaks the prison bars strengthened by society. Faith purifies our perspective on life and lets in love; a good laugh encourages the clear, clean mind and reminds us that love, not hate, makes life work. Faith integrates life; in moments of liberated laughter we sense that integration. Faith brings heaven close; laughter is like an angel opening earth to heaven. Faith drops unnecessary fights and puts us in the right battle; laughter restores the mind to see and the heart to serve God's army. Faith, like gravity, pulls us to the center; laughter supports that pull and helps us see the center with renewed clarity. It does more: it expands our view of life, and that is the genius of its liberating power.

Faith and humor are musts for fruitful living. With them life unfolds its mysterious complexity in portions we can handle. "Humor is essential to any smoothly functioning system of interaction," said a wise man; it is indispensable "to any healthy person, and to any viable group. Humor is, in the last analysis, no joke." One reason is this: humor oils the wheels of life's machinery, and this liberating effect lets God build in us a framework of faith that makes possible saying what needs saying and doing what needs doing.

Robin Williams believes that "comedy is acting out optimism." Optimism is joyous faith alive. It takes off our clothes of fear and re-dresses us in the garb of hope. It melts the tension of frozen anxiety, restores spontaneity, and sees the good in whatever happens.

Paul observed that "where the Spirit of the Lord is, there is freedom" (2 Cor. 3:17). Have you noticed that laughter in a Christian setting not only encourages faith but is also very near the Spirit of God?

2
Laughter Builds Faith

The writer of Psalm 96 sings, "Let the heavens be glad, and let the earth rejoice; let the sea roar, and all that fills it; let the field exult, and everything in it!" (vv. 11–12a). The psalmist goes on in that vein, using the joy of nature to model a happy spirit. Earlier in that psalm, the writer tells us that joyous song is a good vehicle for witnessing to other nations about the glory of God.

Joy and laughter communicate faith, and that happens when we use humor to build up others. To tear down by going for the jugular instead of the jocular vein, as someone put it, stops faith before it gets to its goal. But laughter becomes a means of self-identification; it builds self-image; it alters moods; it serves like a cartoon by getting us to have fun with ourselves; it projects empathy and establishes rapport; it turns negativity into positivity.

On that last point, the matter of positivity, I once asked a college president the secret of his optimism. He gave me three ideas I cannot forget: (1) Decide to be positive; (2) Be positive; (3) Remember that if you lose your optimism, you lose your leadership. Every knowing Christian wants to lead others into positive faith. Whether one is a college president or an unsung Christian helping others in the daily flow of life, these three guidelines give us a clue for working with God in the grand business of propagating the faith.

Add laughter to the college president's three points, and you've got a winning combination! That president does possess a marvelous sense of humor. For decades it has served to strengthen his faith, which consistently issues in positive leadership and influence. Ask anyone who knows him, and you will hear something like this: "Just to be around him makes you stronger."

3

The Contagion
of Humor and Faith

In the Gospels, Jesus heals person after person. The healings can occur because Jesus stimulates faith. Of the woman healed in Matthew 9, Jesus says, "Take heart, daughter; your faith has made you well."

The reverse can also take place. Sneering has the power to rob people of faith, which is why Jesus ordered scoffers out of the room where he was about to bring a girl to life. The scoffers "laughed at" Jesus (Matt. 9:24). Destructive laughter, Jesus knew, destroys faith.

But faith and humor, once married, produce a contagious spirit that has great power for creating good. Thus, when health-care professionals encourage pleasantries, therapy is given a boost. More good news: doctors, nurses, ministers, anybody in the health and wholeness fields, find the nurture of laughter easier in this age of openness. Professionals have historically created an aura rather too solemn and austere to engage in very much humor.

A whole new movement in the medical profession— "gallows humor"—sees mirth designed to cope with death and the constant round of challenges in operating suite and hospital room. One doctor put it this way, "Our humor is a protective device. If we were to talk seriously all the time and act like a bunch of Sir Galahads . . . we just couldn't take all this." Sometimes patients open themselves enough to engage in gallows humor with the health professionals. That puts everybody at ease and assists in activating faith. One researcher even discovered that humor can serve well as a teaching device whereby seasoned doctors, while instructing novices, can help soften the blows of tragedy, initial clinical shock, and the grim realities of suffering.

It is very interesting that the medical community is now beginning to explore the cultivation of humor as a tool of therapy. H. Mindness did a work entitled *Humor and Laughter: Theory, Research, and Applications;* he investigated the uses and abuses of humor in psychotherapy. Another scholar, V. M. Robinson, did a volume on humor in nursing, *Behavioral Concepts and Nursing Intervention,* and produced another work, *Humor and the Health Professions.*

You will notice that Jesus always encouraged faith; he knew its power. Conversely, he dealt forthrightly with any who endangered faith. Well-used pleasantries can put us on Jesus' team and make faith delightfully contagious.

4

Humor, Faith, and Healing

Hebrews 11:1 introduces the classic chapter on faith with these words: "Now faith is the assurance of things hoped for, the conviction of things not seen." The assumption of the entire chapter is that faith can be cultivated. No, not manufactured, for faith is a gift. It is like the body; we ourselves did not make it—God did—but the gift of a good physiology must be cultivated if it is to stay healthy and whole.

One way to keep faith sound is to laugh. In turn, humor becomes the vehicle for passing on health throughout the body. The philosopher Kant said in 1790, long before modern research on fitness and jocularity, that jokes nurture the "vital bodily processes" and generate a "favorable influence on health."

The same is true of psychological well-being. Today we find increasing documentation that humor prevents or helps cure depression. In fact, the whole range of emotions seems touched by laughter. Thus Vera M. Robinson, reporting in Volume II of the *Handbook of Humor Research*, says this: "Certainly, there has been much support for the emotionally therapeutic value of humor as an adaptive, coping behavior, as a catharsis for and relief of tension, as a defense against depression, as a sign of emotional maturity, and as a survival mechanism."

When we feel good, faith comes easier; when we cultivate

faith, we feel better. Herein lies enough reason to release ourselves to laughter, which in turn can release us to fresh faith. W. F. Fry discovered that emotional catharsis parallels physiological response when laughter sets in. He observes that laughter compares to physical exercise, what with oxygen exchange, increase of muscular activity, and the stimulation of the cardiovascular and sympathetic nervous systems. Blood pressure thereby reduces to a healthier level. Fry says that laughter plays its role in preventing heart disease, cerebral vascular accidents, cancer, and other problems.

Researcher after researcher has come up with the good effects of mirth on both body and psyche. The values range from tension reduction to left-brain–right-brain stimulus. The latter principle may someday be used in psychotherapy, because when both hemispheres function, patients have a better chance to see both the logical and abstract phases of their problem.

Faith, healing, and laughter go together. Laughter plays its role by maintaining and enriching the spontaneous belief that can in turn bring welcome healing.

5

Restoring Sanity

After Jesus had identified himself, John comments: "As he [Jesus] spoke thus, many believed in him" (John 8:30). Jesus modeled life and thought at the highest and sanest level. His joy, enthusiasm, belief in people, capacity to face reality (sometimes with humor), all become our criteria for right-mindedness.

When Will Rogers advised, "We are all here for a spell. Get all the good laughs you can," he struck a chord in all of us, the chord that firms up strong, stable thinking. Norman Cousins talks about "that apothecary inside you," by which he means that humor is medicine. When this medicine works, muddled thinking clears like a stirred stream after the sediment settles.

Clarity of mind and active faith are bedfellows, for though the Christian knows the fixed substratum of faith no matter how he or she feels, faith's power is revitalized when the sediment settles. In a sense, faith is sanity. A faith-oriented life functions well on all levels. If humor aids in restoring the balance that is sanity, faith binds life in an integrated working whole.

"Stress" and "burnout" have become everyday words in our fast-paced world. Humor has a way of clearing the psyche so we can see to wash the decks. But it goes further. A Tel Aviv University researcher demonstrated that learning and creativity are greatly enhanced by laughter. Moreover, laughter maximizes memory, he learned. Evidently a merry heart activates the brain and achieves balance and strength.

6

Faith and Comedy

Jesus encouraged us with these familiar words: "In the world you have tribulation; but be of good cheer, I have overcome the world" (John 16:33b).

Comedians help us to be cheerful. They help us come at life with fresh perspective and new faith. Bill Cosby can show us the fun in family problems; Bob Hope helps us poke fun at ourselves; Art Buchwald rescues us from taking the government too seriously. When we can take others, and especially ourselves, without a poker face, we have found a grand secret of liberation and joy. The awful gravity with which we go after success, and the equal pensiveness that accompanies our failures—well, we need to let the air out of those pompous balloons.

Laughter restores clearheaded thinking. That frame of mind brings the Christian back to his faith stance. Without that change, we soon move from seriousness to self-pity, and faith falters just there. Put positively, comedy buoys faith.

Meditative reflection has its place in problem solving and faith building. Solutions usually come with hard thinking. But the character of our reflective times must be free from undue heaviness of spirit. Sometimes, in fact, we must set aside decision making until emotions stabilize. In any event, thinking marked by active faith yields genuine possibilities.

The achieving of that possibility posture is crucial. A walk in the woods may bring it; a phone conversation with an inspiring friend may restore it; a good meal may initiate it. But the astonishing quality of humor is that more often than not, it brings us right back to the place where faith can dominate us, and where, therefore, God can see us meet challenges with poise and success.

7

The Rest of Faith

The classic passage in Isaiah 30 summarizes the soul's rest found in authentic faith: "For thus said the LORD GOD, the Holy One of Israel, 'In returning and rest you shall be saved; in quietness and in trust shall be your strength'" (v. 15).

One of the great but not often heard hymns of the last century came from the knowing pen of Lidie H. Edmunds:

> My faith has found a resting place,
>   Not in device nor creed;
> I trust the Everliving One,
>   His wounds for me shall plead.
>
> *Refrain*
> I need no other argument,
> I need no other plea,
> It is enough that Jesus died,
>   And that he died for me.

The second verse unfolds the security of wholeness in Christ:

> Enough for me that Jesus saves,
>   This ends my fear and doubt;
> A sinful soul I come to him,
>   He'll never cast me out.

111

The final stanza extols the faith that heals:

> My great physician heals the sick,
>   The lost he came to save;
> For me his precious blood he shed,
>   For me his life he gave.

Oswald Chambers caught the point at which security becomes real and joy authentic: "The joy that Jesus gives is the result of our disposition being at one with his own disposition." Chambers suffered ill health and died prematurely, but he knew the "rest of faith" and, therefore, Christian joy. He learned that trying to find his security in circumstances is a dead-end street; he experienced the reality of Isaiah 30:15.

Modern psychotherapy since Carl Jung has known about and encouraged active, secure faith. Jung's famous statement about people who find faith getting well and those who avoid a working faith staying sick—that truth has stuck to our ribs. Christians take Jung a step further to say that in Jesus we find unshakable security and, therefore, the wellness that spells unshakable joy in the depths of our personality.

The very name *Jesus* means wholeness, and wholeness is another name for rest, which is a significant dynamic of joy.

Love, Laughter, and Life

In our life there is a single color, as on an artist's palette, which provides the meaning of life. It is the color of love.

—Marc Chagall

1

The Love
Environment

First John 1:4, interesting for its textual variables, may read either "And we are writing this that our joy may be complete" or ". . . that your joy may be complete." The reason some manuscripts use the word *your* and others *our* may be far more profound than a mere slip of the pen by ancient copyists. The "our" may be due to the atmosphere of fellowship, to the sheer togetherness and free exchange characteristic of the early Christians. After all, love procreates love; when one group extends joy, the very extenders receive joy in their own spirits.

This must suggest the principle behind Mother Teresa's requirement that the corridors and rooms of her healing homes be filled with laughter. Can you imagine! Laughter among the deprived, depressed, distraught? But how wise she is! She knows full well that in a joyful atmosphere, hope, health, and healing take on new impetus. Even the dying capture fresh vision in a happy place.

Leo Buscaglia, in his best-selling *Loving Each Other,* makes this sound statement: "A bond of love is easy to find in an environment of joy." He goes on, "When we laugh together we bypass reason and logic, as the clown does. We speak a universal language. We feel closer to one another."

Of the early Christians, people said, "Behold! how they

love one another." Such an atmosphere! People in all ages have learned, sometimes from rugged trial and error, that glad sharing creates *koinonia*, whereas sad talking develops a counterproductive yield. Who has not watched tensions dissolve in the presence of love, joy, and humor?

2

Love Is a Decision and So Is Joy

When Jesus said to "be perfect, as your heavenly Father is perfect" (Matt. 5:48), He gave us an invitation to fulfillment.

Abraham Lincoln declared, "Most folks are about as happy as they make up their minds to be." In a recent bestselling book on depression, medical doctors Frank Minirth and Paul Meier develop the thesis that *Happiness Is a Choice*. While some critics assess the book as simplistic, there is enough truth in its theme, as in Lincoln's dictum, to make us pause for thought.

But what about joy? For the Christian the presence of Christ, which *is* joy, brings stability through the experiences of life. It is rather like a wheel: the rim goes over the bumpy turf of life's disappointments, but the hub of joy remains firm and steadies the ride. The crunch comes if we allow the hurts of life to inject their poison against the very joy God gives in his Son, Jesus Christ. We have all seen supposedly established Christians leave the Way, or more subtly, keep going to church while nursing destructive emotions such as anger.

Joy is something like love for one's spouse: to maintain it one must make a daily decision. That is analogous to Paul's spirit when he said, ". . . I die every day!" (1 Cor. 15:31). He gave up his "right" to self-sympathy and all the negation that implies.

Concert violinist Itzhak Perlman, though crippled by polio, is a contented man. Asked why, he says he made a decision years ago to look for the happy things in life. He goes on to say others have made the opposite choice: to look for the unpleasant in the world.

Clearly Jesus' "be perfect" implies our ability to decide. The word *perfect* means complete, whole—in everyday language, joyful, happy. It is a major secret of personal fulfillment.

3

Loving Yourself

We often hear with both ears, "Love your neighbor," but frequently only one ear is attuned to those two important words, "as yourself." Jesus expects us to take seriously both parts of the command. Indeed, he knows, even better than modern psychology, that we are projective persons—when we truly love others, we love ourselves, too; when we enjoy self-esteem, we respect others also.

Laughing at ourselves means disarming our perfectionism. As the authors of *Happiness Is a Choice* comment about overcoming depression, "Laughter relaxes us as almost nothing else can. Many individuals improve as soon as they learn no one is perfect (not even they) and as they begin to laugh at their own perfectionistic demands or other shortcomings."

We actually become therapists when we engage ourselves and others in laughter. Luciano de Crescenzo observes, "We are each of us angels with only one wing. And we can only fly embracing each other." Antisocial persons tend to depression, whereas the sociable send out signals of joy and love and appreciate help in flying. As we fly together, we feel good about ourselves and about being in the presence of others.

Miles of research document the simple truth that only those who love can receive love in full measure. Humor not only oils the skids for love; it is a real vehicle of mutual attraction. In an atmosphere of wholesome feedback, it is natural and easier to love ourselves.

Part of the trick lies in the friends we choose. An ambience of easy give-and-take is better than liquor for loosening tongues, creating laughter and the kind of socializing that makes us feel comfortably joyous. By contrast, angry, grouchy people manufacture a disturbing set of vibrations. Getting "in" with the happy people early in life carries far-reaching implications for the development of that healthy mental attitude we call self-respect.

The implications extend to every phase of existence. Leo Buscaglia observes, "When we feel joyful, euphoric, happy, we are more open to life, more capable of seeing things clearly and handling daily tensions." In other words, we relate normally to every dimension—things, persons, God, and of course ourselves. What other everyday basis is there for real self-love and its offspring, joy?

4

Love
One Another

First John, which uses the word *love* nearly half a hundred times, gives us the test of wholeness: "We know that we have passed out of death into life, because we love the brethren . . ." (1 John 3:14). When Jesus told us to love one another as he loves us, he shared the secret of joy-filled living.

The love-one-another theme has captured a good many minds. Commented the ancient writer Statius Caecilius, "They [the Christians] know one another by secret marks and signs, and they love one another almost before they know one another." The modern writer Harry Stack Sullivan says, "When the satisfaction or security of another person becomes as important to one as one's own, then a state of love exists."

Human-behavior research confirms the secret of happiness, personal security, even success: the capacity to relate to others with love and trust. Contrariwise, insecurities, fears, ineptitudes, even mental disease, come by harboring interpersonal feelings that foster anger and mistrust.

One of the practical ways to develop loving rather than negative relationships is simply by taking the initiative to do good things for people. We have this principle modeled in recent findings from an unexpected source, dental research. In the March 1984 issue of the *Journal of the American Dental Association*, K. Seyrek, D.D.S., and Norman Corah, Ph.D., from Buffalo's State University of New York Dental School, tell of getting patients to play video games or watch comedy films during dental procedures. Those who did suffered less pain than even those who simply listened to audio tapes of comedy routines. Why? Distraction, says Dr. Corah. *Prevention* magazine, reviewing the research, reports the conclusion: "Both the video game and the comedy film were better at helping patients transfer their attention to something other than what the dentist was doing."

This experiment illustrates all over again the propensity of the scientific community toward helping, or "loving," people. Concrete ways of loving one another have been put into perspective for Christians by evangelist David Wilkerson: "Love is not only something you feel. It's something you do." As Norman Vincent Peale observes, "Just having enough love in your heart for people to get out there and help them, you will experience exquisite joy and live with enthusiasm and joyous excitement."

In a remarkable book, *Love Is My Meaning,* with a foreword by H.M. Queen Elizabeth, the Queen Mother, there is a lovely passage on the relationship of prayer to helping and loving others. Prayers not only get us into the heart of God, says the writer; they also put us into contact with the need of the world: "It is only as we share God's love and care, however feebly, that we can penetrate beneath the surface in meeting and helping others in their deepest needs. . . ." And when we do that, joy is the inevitable result.

5

The Joy of Loving
Your Spouse

The Bible says a great deal about husbands and wives. For example, there is Ephesians 5, where we read, "Wives, be subject to your husbands" (v. 22) and "husbands should love their wives as their own bodies" (v. 28). Profound happiness awaits couples who follow those prescriptions. The marriage at Cana, at which Jesus performed his first miracle, is an interpretative takeoff center for New Testament marriage-and-family teaching.

The undertone of the Cana story is joy. Marriage is a happy realization. Jesus says something more—it's okay to be happy, to laugh and have fun. Comedians, clowns, and town humorists have their legitimate place, but we can make our own fun. Jesus encouraged the self-generating joy of which all love is an expression.

Current studies imply that a pleasant atmosphere contributes to better interpersonal relationships, including a spirit that enhances homelife. Erma Bombeck, in an interview for *Book Review Digest*, was asked what humor really accomplished. She answered by using the word *everything*, then giving a specific example—marriage. Even when a couple gets to arguing and sees their marriage falling apart—if that couple can bring back the humor—they will stop their gloomy mood and say, "Hey, we're going to be all right." Aunt Erma's wisdom punches holes in our unrelenting preoccupation with problems, a frame of mind that always spawns black thoughts and dismal solutions.

Add an eleventh commandment to your value system: Habitually I will see the delight of life and pass that on to my spouse. I once asked a university president how he kept going. His immediate answer: "Humor." It must have been in a similar context that Lincoln Steffens declared, "The only thing worth having in an earthly existence is a sense of humor." When a marriage gets tough, the tough get it going again with life-changing mirth.

6

Love Life
and Enjoy It!

The apostle Paul quotes Isaiah 64:4 in 1 Corinthians 2:9: "Eye hath not seen, nor ear heard, neither have entered into the heart of man, the things which God hath prepared for them that love him" (KJV). The possibilities of life in Christ are just incalculable. And what releases those possibilities? God Himself, for he brings love and joy, the structural steel for building life abundant.

The prayer of faith believes that. It pierces the hard shell of doubt and unbelief. Unbelief? Yes, that cultural conditioning against happiness. Have you noticed that society tells us we are not supposed to be joyful? That if we experience happiness, we are sure to suffer some reverse?

Couple that underlying feeling with our hesitancy to laugh. I was told at a book-club meeting one evening, after a number of us had occupied ourselves in hearty laughter over a ten- or fifteen-minute period, that I was not supposed to be so mirthful because, "Aren't you a seminary professor?" Our minds, fed on the basic assumption of that question, move into reverse gear when we might enjoy uproarious laughter. We act as though drunks may be uproarious and clowns may release their inhibitions, but if we are to come across as sane and serious about life, we should keep our dignity. What an implied and stultifying definition of dignity!

God expects nature's spontaneity to come out. We all have

a bit of clown in us, some more than others, but we all have it. When we squelch the inner clown, we set up conflicts. We attempt to resolve them by searching outwardly, supposing we will locate life somewhere "out there." That is a mistake, as Sören Kierkegaard saw clearly. The famous Dane showed the positive outworking of his principle. He observed that when a person who "is always turned toward the outside, thinking that his happiness lies outside himself, finally turns inward and discovers that the source is within him"—when that happens—life can come to realization.

Read the New Testament and see that life is in Christ. He is life and he is joy. There are no inhibitions in the Lord—yet dignity comes to its fullest bloom in him. How often he socialized with Mary, Martha, and Lazarus! He walked country roads, admiring the flowers, and he also exposed the legalism of stiff and starchy persons. "Once we realize that Christ was not always engaged in pious talk," says Elton Trueblood in *The Humor of Christ*, "we have made an enormous step on the road to understanding." Trueblood talks about "freeing the Gospel from the excessive sobriety," and when we do that, we make progress in freeing ourselves to love life and engage in its intended joys.

7

How to Restore Love of Life

"Slothfulness casts into a deep sleep . . ." says Proverbs 19:15. That sleep robs life of its buoyant cheer.

In the Middle Ages, the Second Deadly Sin—the one we know as sloth—was called *accidie*. Chaucer refers to "the synne of Accidie." The word is missing in today's unabridged *Webster's*, but we know the phenomenon well.

"Accidie" dictates deep dislike for one's environment—like the nurse who said of her workplace, "I'm fed up with every nook and cranny." Her world had become Dullsville; even the desert would have been better! She was getting nowhere fast and also thought people didn't like her very much. She just wanted to stop work, to relieve herself of concentrating on anything. Her attempts at conversation ended in a downbeat mood.

This is what the French call *ennui*, what we term "boredom." Mind you, this is not mere laziness; in our workaholic age we need occasional do-nothing periods. Perhaps the nurse's trouble was that she worked rather too continuously, without hobbies and reading, or anything to relax her. Whatever the cause of her *ennui*, the reality of her life was a loss of joy; she found herself devoid of the flow of love that yields exhilaration.

How do we go about recovering from accidie, from this sloth that cheats us of life?

1. Since accidie is really a loss of faith in life, tackle faith-building head-on. Confess your "deep sleep" and confess it with honesty. You have already reached second base when you do that much. Then decide for God, others, and yourself all over again. Attitude is always a choice. Never mind how you feel at the moment; settle for life with a positive thrust. Then watch faith grow.

2. Since accidie also relates to others, clear the decks for wholesome relationships. Almost without exception, accidie emerges from some negative interpersonal experience—such as a communication breakdown between you and a family member or a colleague at work. Give your people-problems to God; then observe your mood change for the better. If you must apologize to someone, do it.

3. Since accidie relates to your life goals, renew your dreams. Never mind the broken hopes—all that is history—oil your dream machine with up-to-date purposes for living. Determine to live grandly, largely, to the full. Then know the love of life that is joy.

Slaying Dragons
with the Weapon of Joy

". . . the dragon shalt thou tread under thy feet."

—Book of Common Prayer

Saint George, that swing'd the dragon,
*   and e'er since*
Sits on his horse back at mine hostess' door.

—William Shakespeare
King John

1

Anger, Wrath and Joyous Prayer

In Ephesians 4:31, Paul cries out against "wrath and anger and clamor and slander." Put them away! he admonishes. In their place, he says, put kindness and forgiveness (v. 32). In Colossians 3, he likewise exhorts us to put away "anger, wrath, malice, slander, and foul talk," and to put on "the new nature, which is being renewed in knowledge after the image of its creator" (vv. 8,10).

Paul places anger and wrath side by side to encompass some detrimental emotions. "Wrath" literally means to boil or flame up, as when you put gasoline on green tree cuttings. On the other hand, the word for *anger* means continuous, even habitual or long-lived, vexation. Paul's clear message is to do something about both wrath and anger.

Ancient Greeks likened the wrath that flames up to burning straw—it happens all at once. So, boiling wrath is like a fire in a Kansas wheat field. Paul announces that such flaming rage is sin, a sin of the flesh (Gal. 5:20).

Longstanding anger, like doubt, is a hindrance to prayer (1 Tim. 2:8). That remarkable devotional volume, *God Calling*, entitles the November 1 reading, "Prayer of Joy." "Prayer can be like incense, rising ever higher and higher," begins the reading—"or it can be like a low earth-mist clinging to the ground, never once soaring." A lifestyle of anger hinders prayer. "But the prayer of real faith is the prayer of

Joy, that sees and knows the heart of Love it rises to greet, and that is so sure of a glad response." The Book of James tells us to stay away from anger (long-range) because God's righteousness has a hard time thriving in that vengeful atmosphere (1:19–20). And Jesus warns that this kind of anger erupts in calling people names and hurling insults; such behavior in turn prompts the judgment of God (Matt. 5:22) and does not encourage a glad spirit.

2

Joy and Some Research Findings

Psalms 65 and 66, in *Today's English Version*, come at life with joy as a basic assumption. Hear, for example, Psalm 65:12–13: "The pastures are filled with flocks; the hillsides are full of joy. The fields are covered with sheep; the valleys are full of wheat. Everything shouts and sings for joy." The first three verses of Psalm 66 pick up the same motif: "Praise God with shouts of joy, all people! Sing to the glory of his name; offer him glorious praise! Say to God, 'How wonderful are the things you do! Your power is so great that your enemies bow down in fear before you.'"

We now know from research that a joyful attitude generates good health, staves off oncoming illness, and provides coping strength to get goals achieved. Take, for example, the research findings recorded in *USA Today* for August 26, 1985: "Personality affects immune cell strength, which influences whether people become sick or not. . . ." The findings, reported to an American Psychological Association meeting in Los Angeles, are indeed newsworthy, but they only reflect a fundamental posture of Scripture.

"Tests on the immune system show that it's not stress," the report goes on, "but our way of responding to it that triggers illness." The psalmist might have groused about the hard work of farming and the reverses brought by nature. Instead, he praises God for His role in productivity.

In one study, 190 medical students submitted to research. Those who looked gloomily at exam time suffered less immunity and more illness; those who saw the experience as challenge, rather than threat, heightened their immune ability.

A five-year study of some fifty-five Three Mile Island residents (near Harrisburg, Pennsylvania) showed that the presence of threat from the nearby nuclear reactor lowered physical immune capacity and increased stress-linked hormones. In other words, the threat seemed to be a greater deterrent to health than the actual nuclear accident.

Still another research project reported in the *USA Today* article relates to herpes patients. Those who are depressed wrestle with "significantly more recurrences of the disease" than the optimistic. They also show lower immune-cell function than the positive-minded people. More, the thirty-six patients studied demonstrated a decline in immune-cell stamina just prior to a herpes attack.

Entertaining the dragon of fear may result in illness or failure; that in turn rears the head of another dragon, anger. Contrariwise, joy, optimism, and positivity spell faith, which in turn writes itself in our minds and our very body chemistry.

3

Three Dragons and Money

Jesus admonished us to develop "treasures in heaven," adding that earthbound riches have a way of yielding disappointment, whereas eternal investments bring joy (Matt. 6:19–21).

On the surface, Jesus' statement, about laying up treasures in heaven instead of earth, looks incongruous. Yet, we know greed's results. As William Barclay says, "The strange thing about the sin of avarice and the desire for money is that we think about it, and when we see what it means, we wonder how anyone could be such a fool as to be guilty of it!" But everyone wants to get rich, and even morally responsible people would like to see if they can acquire wealth while avoiding the pitfalls.

Money has, through the centuries, given rise to a great deal of joke telling. We attempt to cope with life's inconformabilities by laughter. And when one recognizes the angers, guilts, and fears generated by stocks, bonds, and inheritances, who would say humor cannot help us deal with the emotional involvements related to such money matters?

But what is the underlying tension between eternal investment and worldly greed? Since greed never satisfies itself, the desire for money becomes a god. The fruit of all that can only be anger, eventually fear, and also guilt. The cure? Reducing desire to proper size by a generous, openhanded spirit. Have you noticed the liberated delight in persons who love to give?

Money studies show that a substantial raise in salary brings adjustment problems, for example in marriage and family. Sometimes those problems prove severe and even lead to breaking up a home. While the implications of such research are multiple, one factor makes itself especially felt: overextended desire contributes to maladjustment.

Do you remember the children's story about the man who wanted everything he touched to become gold? He got his wish. His eyes lighted with excitement as he touched eggs and watched them turn into money. One thing after another glittered and glistened as he put a finger or hand on them. Then he got hungry, but when bread and meat became gold— well, he couldn't eat yellow metal, no matter how precious. The greedy man begged for a return to things as they were.

Joy in life resides not in *getting* so much as in *giving*. That is why Jesus said it is more blessed to give than to receive. And *blessed* is an old-fashioned word for "happiness," which has a way of coming to those whose angers are redeemed, whose fears are healed, and whose guilts are forgiven.

4

"Primary Reactions" and the Attitude of Joy

The apostle Paul said we should have no anxiety about anything, but in everything, with prayer and thanksgiving, make our wishes known to God. He goes on to assure us that, with this spirit, God's peace will invade our hearts. Even Paul lacks the ability to spell out the depth of this peace; he calls it a calm that "transcends all understanding" (Phil. 4:7, NIV).

Ella Wheeler Wilcox fights fear in this language:

> Fate used me meanly; but I looked at her and laughed,
> That none might know how bitter was the cup I quaffed.
> Along came Joy, and paused beside me where I sat,
> Saying, 'I came to see what you were laughing at.'

The southern humorist Lewis Grizzard uses less-dignified language to describe his reaction to anxiety. He wrote a book, after his heart surgery, entitled *They Tore Out My Heart and Stomped That Sucker Flat* (1982).

The science of physiological psychology can measure accelerated or retarded pulse, diminished or increased glandular activity, temperature changes in the body—any of which can stimulate body parts and in turn trigger emotions. And the strongest emotions? Most researchers answer: fear, anger, and love. These are sometimes called the three "primary reactions." Any of the three can be activated from outward circumstances (external stimuli) or internal thoughts (subjective stimuli). Memory, association, or introspection have power to start the flow of fear, anger, or love. John Watson, a pioneer in psychological studies, demonstrated that even infants can experience the three primary emotions.

Another of the pioneer researchers, William James, spoke specifically on what we can do about these emotional reactions: "The greatest discovery of my generation is that human beings can alter their lives by altering their attitudes of mind." We know from experience and intuition, and from scientific laughter studies, that humor is one of nature's instruments for altering attitudes. Thus, the call to action looms clear enough: engage your psyche with the positives of life, then watch the mind's atmosphere change and, in turn, one's whole frame of reference.

5

How Do You Perceive Reality?

Jesus taught us that "The eye is the lamp of the body. So, if your eye is sound, your whole body will be full of light; but if your eye is not sound," He concludes, "your body will be full of darkness." He even says, "If then the light in you is darkness, how great is the darkness!" (Matt. 6:22–23).

Jesus here talks about the basis of perceived reality. We all see life as essentially friendly or unfriendly, sad or glad, full of disappointment or opportunity. Jesus announces that a happy or unhappy view of life comes from what we see. The practical implication is that we must *choose* good things to look at.

Have you noticed that people who do not believe in happy marriages associate with persons who have a twisted view of family? Likewise, individuals who cannot accept God as a loving heavenly Father identify with those who do not see God as a personal being. By the same token, all who perceive life as a dirty deal develop a circle of friends who live angry lives.

Psychologists have long known that environment can generate anger or any of the emotions. Fear, anger, and resentment cause biochemical changes and, if the negative emotions persist, give rise to behavioral and bodily changes. For example, anger can speed up heart action, send the body into shaking motions, cause temporary blindness or loss of voice. Some grapple with their emotions by putting on a mask of bravado or of false humility.

Jesus says No to escapist ways of handling reality. Change your friends and setting, He exhorts. Yes—for the people you are with determine what you see. And what you see shapes your style of perceiving. A joy-filled environment has enormous healing power.

6

Joy Fights Bitterness

Jesus, whose forthright communication has a way of getting through to us, said that His words were intended to make us full of joy (John 15:11). The post-biblical writer Hermas caught something of the meaning of Jesus' words when he exhorted, "Put sadness away from thee, for truly sadness is the sister of half-heartedness and bitterness." He says more:

> Array thee in the joy that always finds favour in God's sight and is acceptable with him; yea, revel thou therein. For everyone that is joyous worketh and thinketh those things that are good, and despiseth sadness. But he that is sad doth always wickedly; first because he maketh sad the Holy Spirit that hath been given to man for joy; and secondly he worketh lawlessness, in that he neither prays to God nor gives thanks.

Then Hermas comes to his clinching point with a challenge: "Therefore cleanse thyself from this wicked sadness, and thou shalt live with God. Yes, unto God all they shall live who have cast out sadness from themselves, and arrayed themselves in all joy."

What strikes us immediately about this ancient statement is the relation of sadness to wickedness, of the role of the

141

Holy Spirit in cleansing. The practicality of these second-century words help us fight bitterness with joy.

Sadness and bitter feelings can flower from self-sympathy. A woman who lost her husband of a heart attack before retirement developed a chronic bitterness. She nursed the trauma, told God he was unfair, and coddled her anger. Result? A personality change. Whereas she had previously lived a loving and outgoing life, never knowing an enemy, now she withdrew into anger. She actually truncated her usefulness and cut off her own peace of mind. Joy has the power to reverse that.

The tricky thing about trauma like the widow's is that it comes unawares. How, then, do we prepare for it? By cultivating in good days joy, laughter, and mirth, some of God's chief instruments for faith development. Faith, like a muscle, builds girth as we school ourselves in positive attitudes. And one of the best ways to strengthen strong spirits is to fight difficulty with deliberate joy. Note that Hermas even says to "revel" in joy.

7

How to
Handle Guilt

Jeremiah 48:33 reveals the judgment of God:

> Gladness and joy have been taken away
>   from the fruitful land of Moab;
> I have made the wine cease from the wine presses;
>   no one treads them with shouts of joy;
>   the shouting is not the shout of joy.

God's judgment is here depicted as the removal of joy.

Moab simply would not face her guilt. Just there lies the reason for the absence of delight in her life.

Of course, there are two kinds of guilt in our modern world: real and imagined. Fancied guilt comes from either a too-conscientious spirit or a twisted mind. Laughter can assist in putting our merely supposed guilts to rest. But real guilt, as Moab experienced, needs forthright confession and the accompanying willingness to make amends.

Laughter, of course, will not erase wrongdoing. One of the subtle tragedies of our time is what we may call "covering laughter," laughter that attempts to persuade people to believe that wrong is right and vice versa. Modern drama, telecommunications, and cinema will have much to answer for at judgment day!

The clear message of the Scriptures from beginning to end is simply this: the guiltless have joy; the guilty suffer dejection. Sad or glad? That's a basic biblical question. And what is unique to biblical theology is the heartening promise that the guilty need not stay that way. More, when God forgives our guilt, He forgets it and we can, too.

One more piece of the picture: Moab refused to admit her guilt. Such pretense yields rotten fruit—maladjustment. The tricky factor is that Moab thought she could get away with sin (Jer. 48). She found out differently.

Willingness to see the whole picture is the launching pad for confession, which in turn gives birth to fresh beauty and gladness.

Communication
with Joy

Humor is essentially social. When we hear a joke, we immediately want to tell it to others. When we enjoy a joke in an audience situation, we tend to turn to our fellows and share our enjoyment with them.

—Robert T. Oliver
The Psychology of Persuasive Speech

1

You Yourself

Psalm 57 is the cry of a man hurting deeply: "I cry to God Most High. . . . He will send from heaven and save me. . . . God will send forth his steadfast love and his faithfulness!" (vv. 2–3). The clear note of joy and faith rings right through David's misery. He is realistic but not self-sympathizing.

Helen Hayes and her husband, Charles MacArthur, lost their nineteen-year-old daughter to polio. Charlie died a few years later, but Helen Hayes has lived productively into her eighties. Her own explanation is that Charlie never quit asking, "Why should it happen to us? We didn't do anything to anybody. We never hurt anybody. Why? Why? Why?" Helen, seeing other people in tragedy, asks, "Why *not* us?"

The complexities of human nature and thought outstrip our abilities to analyze, much less judge. So, whether the great actress was right or wrong we cannot know, but surely she was correct in insisting on a positive attitude.

One's basic attitude comes through in communication. Some people can mask their real attitudes, but not for long. Most of our communication is through body language, what the professionals call kinesics. Another part is tone. The least impactful element is language, the actual words. Since body language and tone do not submit to rehearsal so easily as words, kinesics and tonics are unconscious instruments of self-disclosure. They subtly reveal our identity. What we *are* communicates first, last, and loudest.

Helen Hayes's basic joy comes through, even as she relates her tragedy. Her very manner tells us much about her positivism.

The ethical character of a communicator carries enormous weight. The incarnation of Christ is an eloquent example, and that is why S. D. Gordon said, "Jesus is God spelling himself out in language that man can understand." The bottom line: we trust Jesus because we know his integrity.

When Phillips Brooks defined preaching as truth through personality, he articulated the incarnational principle of communication. When the psalmist says right out that he's hurting, God respects that honesty. When Helen Hayes reveals her faith, she exposes her heart and therefore communicates fully.

S. D. Gordon, author of more than twenty devotional books, sums up in one simple sentence the principle that you yourself communicate: "The way from God to a human heart is through a human heart." When human hearts are joy-filled, they communicate with peculiar power.

2

Enthusiasm

Proverbs 15:23 puts rich meaning and truth in this language: "To make an apt answer is a joy to a man, and a word in season, how good it is!" When we say the right thing at the right time, delight and enthusiasm characterize our communication.

Norman Vincent Peale poses a question: Why are some writers, speakers, and leaders remembered forever? "For their ability, leadership qualities and achievements, of course," he begins, then adds, "but one important reason is their boundless enthusiasm and the joy they took in life and in the world."

"Enthusiasm" literally means to be inspired or possessed by God. When we talk about inspired speech, we mean that stimulus is heightened. The ancients saw that as godly. God is indeed in our communication when we rouse others to think noble thoughts and stir themselves to good deeds.

Listen to what three different Samuels say about enthusiasm. Samuel Chadwick, the English Methodist preacher: "Men ablaze are invincible. The stronghold of Satan is proof against everything but fire." Samuel Goldwyn, movie producer: "Enthusiasm is the key not only to the achievement of great things but to the accomplishment of anything that is worthwhile." Finally, Sam Jones, the American evangelist: "A horse that will pull on a cold collar will do to depend on—and the best Christians are those who never need 'warming up.'"

Those three snippets symbolize a whole literature of enthusiasm in the Western World. Animated address has a contagion about it. In fact, very ordinary things can be said in a framework of delighted animation, and they will carry genuine thrusts of meaning.

Enthusiasm and joy are Siamese twins. One cannot move without the other. The two can be either quiet or outgoing in manner, but they will create momentum. When the Spirit of God is the Author of that enthusiasm and joy, they set hearts afire, and in that flame mere words are translated into reality. And that is communication.

Robert Murray McCheyne cries, "O Lord, evermore give us this enthusiasm!" Another son of Scotland, James S. Stewart, spoke with equal fervor: "The supreme need of the church is the same in the twentieth century as in the first; it is men on fire for Christ." Have you noticed that wherever you encounter that mood of enthusiasm, the joy of the Lord is present?

3

Communication Overload

The classic passage on God's communication with Elijah finds summary in these cogent words: "And behold, the LORD passed by, and a great and strong wind rent the mountains, and broke in pieces the rocks before the LORD, but the LORD was not in the wind; and after the wind an earthquake, but the LORD was not in the earthquake; and after the earthquake a fire, but the LORD was not in the fire. . . ." Then comes the unexpected: "and after the fire a still small voice" (1 Kings 19:11b–12). Everyone knows the quiet voice was God's.

The *Superwoman* news sheet recently came to life in retaliation against "rock-breaking winds," those current fire-and-earth communiques, all saying today's woman can be super everything. She can smell like a flower garden twenty-four hours a day, rear children without emotional hang-ups, keep her husband happy, work fifty hours a week or more, and maintain her equilibrium through it all. *Superwoman* says No to all that. It says women must find quiet spaces in their lives if they expect to keep their balance. It's okay to go around without a burden of guilt that something is undone.

Both men and women, and now children, have succumbed to our twentieth-century communication overload, no doubt in reaction to an earlier era when so many were just plain lazy and chaotic in lifestyle. Today our problem is not only different but doubled in intensity. The very vehicles of communication announcing we can be superpersons clamor for attention with rock-breaking earthquake sounds and flashing signals of fire. A kind of rock-and-roll bombast characterizes the TV commercials, the garish highway signboards, the loud and fast-talking radio ads.

But God's communications are often quiet. We can find them in the touch of a little child's hand, the awesome stillness of a wooded hiking trail, a silent sunrise, a book by a winter's fire, the inner voice. What strikes the listener attuned to God's voice is the comfort, strength, and joy that always accompany it.

4

Should I Use Humor in Speeches?

The Book of Proverbs has a great deal to say about speech. Whether the advice is private or public, the passages sum up this way: speech must be both appropriate and wise.

There are certain "appropriate and wise" ways to employ humor when addressing the public. When a good laugh puts your audience at ease, a bridge is constructed. Rapport is especially important if either audience or speaker feels ill at ease for any reason.

The best wit in one-on-one situations flows out of an ordinary conversational mode. By the same token, that's what will work best in public settings. If, for example, you tell jokes well, you are probably a sure ringer for telling them to a group. But woe to the leader who can't tell funny stories but tries anyway!

Both Steve Allen and Art Linkletter warn against using off-color jokes. After all, there is an element of judgment required in sharing stories—and not just "dirty" stories. One must use critical faculties when sizing up the background and setting of the audience (church, school, club, whatever), the occasion (humor at a funeral? rarely), group mood (if they are already laughing, you may be able to hitchhike on the atmosphere). "Fitness" is crucial: when the feel of a story or humor line fits like your hand in a glove, you've got a winner.

Playful kidding ("roasting"), often an in-thing today, must

be used cautiously and with reserve, since it depends on your own gifts as a public person and the dignity of the person you are ribbing. You don't kid the university dean unless he, you, and the circumstances permit it. "Authenticity" is the key to successful public humor. If your joke or real-life story has the ring of truth about it, if it meshes with reality, people identify and respond appropriately. If, on the other hand, artifice comes through, if the audience gets the idea you have calculated your measured phrases just to get a laugh, the reaction will reflect displeasure.

Above all, let your humor suggest the joy Christians know. The essence of the early Christian witness was radiance. It was said of one godly person, "His smiles were fraught with greater meaning than his sermons."

5

Communication for Learning

The Bible is full of exhortation to learn. Knowledge, when married to wisdom, yields the rewards of joy and fulfillment. The Bible writers would be pleased with the advances in twentieth-century education, not only in terms of information, but inspiration as well.

The "dangerous nonsense" decried by Neil Postman, in *Amusing Ourselves to Death: Public Disclosure in the Age of Showbusiness*, would be equally censured by Scripture writers. After all, we do need to think clearly. Television, this New York University professor of communications believes, has made American talk "shriveled and absurd" and is reducing our culture to mere entertainment.

What the Bible would not agree with is the oft-heard statement in our time that culture and learning cannot advance in an era of pictures. The Bible itself is a pictographic book. Modern brain research documents that the vast majority of people do picture-thinking, and that this is the way most things are learned. Abstraction, in general, does not initiate learning well.

Actually, education has done a turnabout. Educators once came at their task only with great seriousness; now we know that learning can be fun as well as serious in intent. Researchers have discovered teachers from the elementary level to graduate school using humor, film, games—all sorts of fun vehicles—as means toward measurable learning. Educational TV is the most obvious example of the learning-can-be-fun movement.

Research demonstrates that schoolchildren may listen and learn better in the presence of humor. Fast-paced humor proved, in some research, a better vehicle for capturing adolescents' attention. TV, books, and magazines can all use humor to educational advantage. But humor excels in video learning, where the stimulus to laugh works with musical background and entertainment props as support mechanisms. Situations and circumstances differ, of course, and much research is still to be done. But Dolf Zillmann and Jennings Bryant—in "Uses and Effects of Humor in Educational Ventures," a chapter in Volume II of the *Handbook of Humor Research*—indicate not only the complexities of humor usage in learning, but also that well-used humor can be a facilitator of genuine education.

6

A Way of
Communicating Help

The apostle Paul, in his prison Epistle, Philippians, uses words like "joy," "thanks," "rejoice." As it turns out, that little book is a cogent ministry, especially to people in a bind of some sort.

Humor can fill people with joy and thus be genuine ministry. For example, every human being feels at some time or another the aggression people use to get their own way. The heaviness of that feeling can be diffused by a story or a single line that elicits laughter. For example, little children get pretty demanding. One might tell the W. C. Fields pun: "Mr. Fields," he was supposed to have been asked, "do you believe in clubs for children?"—"Only when kindness fails," he replied.

Again, humor is a marvelous balm when life's contradictions shackle us. To reduce the heaviness of incongruities to manageable size is a great service. "It's not the passages in Scripture I cannot understand that bother me," said Mark Twain; "it's the passages I do understand that trouble me." Mark Twain had a way of making fog go away, while at the same time facing up to life's conundrums.

Think about humor as emotional release from the mounting tensions of life. One suspects that parties, at base, are created to help us handle stress. And parties are known for gaiety. Sometimes that gaiety is advanced more simply by sharing funny experiences.

When my daughter Cherith, but three or four at the time, asked her mother if she could invite the little girl next door to play in the sandbox, Kathleen replied, "Yes, of course." Kathleen listened to the little playmates in the sandbox. She could hear clearly from the kitchen, where she watched the two girls from the open window. Presently the three-year-old from next door asked Cherith, "Is your daddy really a doctor?" (The little one had apparently heard students, from the college where I taught, call me "Doctor.") "Yep," said Cherith, "he's the kind of doctor that can't help anybody." When I get to taking myself too seriously, I think of that incident.

7

Laughter
as Communication

Laughter studies, as we think of them today, are of only recent origin. Psychologists began such inquiries in 1928, and theologians have also done some research and writing in the last few years. Philologists are probably the most recent to enter the arena. But one thing they all seem to agree on is this: laughter, at root, is a method of communication.

And a powerful medium it can be. Jesus' comment about the log and the speck (Matt. 7:5), a species of humor called irony, tells us about judging. It says that guilty people love to divert attention away from their own sins by pointing out the mistakes of others.

Dickens's ingenious description of London's fog-and-smoke covering is really a way of exposing not the evils of coal burning (the clean-air movement was yet to come), but what George F. Will of the *Washington Post* calls the "choking legal system" of the day. People who see behind the figure cannot help but smile at its relevance.

Or take Oscar Wilde's scathing play, *The Importance of Being Earnest*, his masterpiece of 1895. Here, the hypocrisy and raw inconsistencies of society are uncovered for all to see, much to the delight of theatergoers. Wilde intended to expose appearance for appearance's sake, to ridicule people who take trivial matters seriously, and to put sincerity and earnestness

159

into perspective. The play is very funny, as Wilde meant it to be.

Jesus, Dickens, and Wilde tell us that when people cannot hear by direct communication, indirect talk, especially when coated with the frosting of humor, can make truth palatable. Let's face it: when something tastes good it goes down easier.

The Joy
of Creativity

*Claudel, the French poet, said after listening to
Beethoven's Fifth Symphony that he knew now
that at the heart of the universe there was joy.*

—Gerald Kennedy

1

The Freedom to Create

Saint Paul writes, "Now the Lord is the Spirit, and where the Spirit of the Lord is, there is freedom" (2 Cor. 3:17). Paul might have ended the verse this way, ". . . there is freedom and creativity," for where the Spirit of the Lord is, both appear.

Plautus, a Roman playwright who lived before Christ, paints a clown in his drama *Pseudolus*. The buffoon (Pseudolus) has red hair, a potbelly, legs like a piano, a big head, pointed eyes, darkish skin, very large feet, and a red face. Although Pseudolus is a slave, in the play he enjoys absolute freedom. Superior to his master, he is the writer, analogous to the real writer, Plautus. In the monologue of act one, he puts pen to paper and creates a plot. "I'll play the playwright," he shouts in the spirit of freedom and fun.

That freedom to imagine is the seed of great joy. Actually, to imagine constructively results in multiplied joy and is the base of much humor. An important difference between Christian and secular humor, however, relates to freedom's boundaries. The Christian is not free to unleash human impulses at will, for twisted drives find their rootage in evil. Making light in implied approval of drink, promiscuity, violence, or other evil results ultimately not in creativity but in disaster. To laugh at God's laws is final imprisonment.

On the other hand, to poke innocent fun at our weak-

163

nesses—to employ surprise, incongruity, and exaggeration, to allow sanctified imagination to roam for joy and build for character development—that is authentic liberty and brings not a sour but a happy taste to one's spirit.

To assume the freedom offered in Christ to innovate in the daily round, the workplace, the recreation setting—that is to set the stage for optimum fulfillment.

2

Music from a Cheerful Heart

The frequently quoted Proverbs 15:13 fits Franz Joseph Haydn perfectly: "A glad heart makes a cheerful countenance, but by sorrow of heart the spirit is broken." Haydn declared, "God gave me a cheerful heart, so He will surely forgive me if I serve Him cheerfully."

"The music of Haydn," says one authority, "has cheer, beauty, logic, order, nobility, freshness of imagination, and humor." Little wonder his works appear on concert programs with frequency.

What accounts for such fundamental joy in the great composer's scores? The answer, simple yet profound, goes right to the heart of God and creation. Haydn perceived God as sovereign; he saw nature as not chaotic but ordered. Thus the superficial and transient glamor, tragedy, and excitements of the world carried little weight with Franz Joseph.

But Haydn got his foundational philosophy from the Bible. That Book must be the basis of everything, he believed—the basis of politics, religion, education, one's entire lifestyle. To accept the scriptural rationale for all of life was to find freedom; to deny that basis was to put oneself in prison.

The great composer did not use that theological basis as an escape device, as some have tried to do in the crises of life. Rather, he faced his difficulties. In them God gave him cheer, and from the commingling of tragedy and joy his music flowed in a never-ending stream of creativity.

As a boy studying music, Haydn was full of pranks and fun. On one occasion he simply could not say No to the temptation to cut off the pigtail of a singer in the choir. He was ousted, but he never lost his child's heart for mirth. His music documents that humor.

But so many things militated against the maintenance of Haydn's merriment. Composition was always hard for him, but his disciplined regularity overcame what could easily have developed into laziness. His wife could bear no children; and, almost as bad, she had absolutely no appreciation for her husband's work. Would you believe she used his manuscripts for pastry papers and hair curlers?

Out of all this came an original, the giant who created the formats for symphony and string quartet as we know them today. Mozart gave him the right nickname, "Papa Haydn."

Franz Joseph's aim was not to make a big new splash in the musical world; he simply wanted to make people happy. He wished to help people substitute a smile for a frown, to see their disappointments through fresh eyes.

He sensed God's hand on his own as he composed. Daily, as he put together the *Creation*, "I fell on my knees and asked God for strength." In 1808, now an old man, Haydn heard a public performance of the *Creation*. When the mighty chorus rendered, "And There was Light," Haydn's hands lifted heavenward and he whispered, "Not from me. It all comes from above."

And just there lies the Source of all that is good, including a cheerful and creative heart.

3

The Joy of
Creative Answers

She was technically a good tennis player, but something was missing. The instructor, a creative spirit, studied her game and then came up with a suggestion that proved innovative and timely. He asked, "Do you know 'The Blue Danube Waltz'?" She did. "Then, as we play, I want you to time your strokes to the rhythm of 'The Blue Danube Waltz.'"

She hummed the tune as she volleyed. Her forehand and backhand began to find their tempo. Then her movements flowed! Flowed, I suspect, rather like a ballet dancer's.

When she stopped, joy was written on her face, says Norman Vincent Peale in telling the remarkable results. She exclaimed, "I never felt the joy and thrill of this game before. For the first time in my life I feel I can master it." A creative idea had helped her find her own rhythm and harmony and, therefore, an improved game.

The Living Bible renders Galatians 5:22–23 like this: "But when the Holy Spirit controls our lives he will produce this kind of fruit in us: love, joy, peace, patience, kindness, goodness, faithfulness, gentleness and self-control. . . ." The Spirit's control is the basis of creativity, and the origin of sound problem solving. And the inward result? Satisfaction, the joy Paul describes.

I have a friend with another kind of problem: high blood pressure, the result of his very busy executive life. When he is pulled in more directions than he feels comfortable handling, he sometimes goes fishing. Driving thirty miles into the nearby mountains, he stops his car at a favorite spot, pulls on his wading boots, takes rod and reel into the river, and forgets his problems. The gentle lapping of the waters against the shore, the never-ending flow of the river, the song of the birds, the wind in the trees—the whole mix of outdoor experience restores him.

One day, after fishing in the mountains, he went to the doctor. The physician's astonished look matched his comments: "Your blood pressure is nearly normal." The physician wanted to know if the hard-working executive went fishing often enough! A good question, for this creative solution, born of God's own creativity, restored my friend's own creative potential.

As he told me all about this, the tone of joy in his voice and the look of delight on his face led me to believe he would go fishing again and again.

4

The Joy of Creative Closure

The close of Book IV of the Psalms reads like this: "Blessed be the LORD, the God of Israel, from everlasting to everlasting! And let all the people say, 'Amen!' Praise the LORD!" (Ps. 106:48). Actually, quite a number of the psalms end in similar fashion, not always in doxology, but often with the special sense of closure that reflects joyous fulfillment.

What we must notice is this: as frequently as a psalm terminates in closure, the body of the chapter has struggled with an issue—usually a warring crisis in battle or in the soul. The reader can watch the dialogue of the psalmist, then see him come to a creative conclusion by the power of God's Spirit.

That dialogical pattern with a final resolution models the mind's workings. Blaise Pascal observed the Yes-No-Final Answer movement of the mind in problem solving; he informed us that this is the way God made us to handle challenges. That interior conversation is also one way we create, for all creativity is really problem solving.

Now here's the sticky wicket: the dialogue can be so stimulating that we rob ourselves of the sheer joy of coming to decisions. Take the matter of a new job. What delight there really is in a fresh environment, different colleagues, perspectives on work not thought of before. The whole change of coloration holds potential for gladdening the heart. Yet we miss that

169

if we merely ask questions *ad infinitum* and never really decide for the new employment.

Neurosis is indecision. Therapists are aware of the negative impact of uncertainty. This is not to say we should engage in careless decision making. To the contrary, the more we involve ourselves in the hard business of clear thinking, the greater the joy when at last we come down on the point of closure.

5

The Art
of the Child

Jesus, sharing with his disciples who had asked about greatness, said, "Truly, I say to you, unless you turn and become like children, you will never enter the kingdom of heaven. Whoever humbles himself like this child, he is the greatest in the kingdom of heaven" (Matt. 18:2–4).

In the whole of his thirty-five years, Wolfgang Amadeus Mozart never lost the little child in him. His playful mind was constantly creating. He could not think of mundane things like running a household; he filled his head with rhythms, notations, harmonies, sequences, motifs. With the excitement of a little child getting ready to go on a journey, he put his creations on score paper.

Musicologists agree that Mozart had more music in him than any other composer. God made him to create. Songs, rhythms, and variations fairly leaped from his brain onto paper. The graceful, dancelike character of his compositions have made him the most popular composer of all time. "Composing," he confessed, "is my one joy and passion."

Mozart had fun with his public. He loved watching reactions to his music. The gliding grace of his sounds, tones, and rhythms slid right into the hearts of his listeners, lifted them to new heights and left them saying, "Life's a happy affair after all."

Wolfgang Amadeus would probably have been diagnosed

today as a hyperactive. He simply could not sit still or keep quiet. He sang, jumped about, rollicked with laughter, even when others could see no humor. His genius absorbed everything musical—compositional forms, national norms, cultural overtones—and this mix translated into grand sounds. He wrote so much that it is doubtful whether any music lover has actually listened carefully to all his compositions.

Father of the modern concerto, Mozart was also the first to perform a piano concerto publicly. But whether he played or wrote, he came across as a singer. Song was the center of his creativity, especially in his later years. He loved to write in the garden, listening to the songbirds. He used varied colors of ink on his scores. The transparency of his music is like a clear running brook.

Mozart loved life. He wrote *The Marriage of Figaro*, which established the comic opera for time to come, and for him opera lent itself to the humor and excitement he saw in life. "I never lie down at night," said this genius, "without reflecting that, young as I am, I may not live to see another day. Yet no one of all my acquaintances could say that in company I am morose or disgruntled. For this blessing I daily thank my Creator."

The source and center of his faith was that Creator. Although Mozart is sometimes portrayed as without much faith, his aim was to reflect God. And the joy of the Almighty's creation shines through unclouded. Like a little child, Mozart never got over the wonder of God's world. Even though we cannot write music like Mozart, we can cultivate his sense of wonder, source of joyous creativity, in whatever we do.

6

Creativity
and Disappointments

In a great, grand passage on the redemption of Israel, Jeremiah burst into divinely inspired song: "Then shall the maidens rejoice in the dance, and the young men and the old shall be merry. I will turn their mourning into joy, I will comfort them, and give them gladness for sorrow" (Jer. 31:13).

Ludwig van Beethoven, keenly aware of God's sovereignty in the midst of sorrow, saw the Almighty as his comfort, authority, and source of talent. He prayed on one occasion that he felt "called upon to produce" music. "Divine One," he cried, "thou lookest into my inmost soul, thou knowest it, thou knowest that love of man and desire to good live therein."

Yet Beethoven lived a tragic life. Deafness turned him inward. A nephew he tried to rear with tenderness and love turned out poorly. Ludwig was a loner by nature. But somehow none of these things kept him from composing marvelously exuberant music. Frank Gaebelein, in his excellent essay, "Beethoven: A Bicentennial Tribute," observes that because Beethoven "translated his Job-like experience into tone, musical literature has no more profound statement of the problem of suffering and its resolution than his."

Then Gaebelein relates the powerful story of Geoffery Bull, English missionary tortured by the Chinese Communists. Bull says that even though his captors robbed him of his

Bible and made him face the possibility of death, when Beethoven's *Emperor Concerto* came wafting into his cell from a nearby radio, it brought such refreshment that the prisoner could confront anything. The gripping story comes from Bull's well-known *When Iron Gates Yield*.

Ludwig could write lively scherzos (*scherzo* means "joke"). He could put witticisms into music; his rondos are famous for that. He also expressed struggle, of course. Similar to the Book of Psalms, Beethoven ranged over the human stretches of life and emotion, which explains why the man and his works are so universally loved.

One authority summarizes Beethoven's music and the joy it brings with incisive accuracy: ". . . as you listen . . . thank God for this man whose music speaks so eloquently of struggle with affliction, of the joy and humor of life, or sorrow and consolation, and serenity that surmounts suffering."

Art, like humor, is often born in adversity. People who use their disappointments as instruments of creativity bring joy not only to themselves but to others. One mother in constant pain helped start a Christian day school, and she herself taught in it. No one could be around her without knowing she was genuinely happy.

7

God's Creativity

The classic Ezekiel passage on the valley of bones speaks of these bones as "very dry"—"Can these bones live?" is the crucial question (Ezek. 37:2–3). The answer: "Thus says the LORD GOD to these bones: Behold, I will cause breath to enter you, and you shall live" (v. 5).

Have you noticed God's creative genius in continually bringing life out of death, order out of chaos, good out of evil? Mother Teresa says God uses us to bring about his creative products. How? By

> loving as He loves,
> helping as He helps,
> giving as He gives,
> serving as He serves,
> rescuing as He rescues,
> being with Him for all the twenty-four hours,
> touching Him in His distressing disguise.

That "distressing disguise" is the clincher. When Mother Teresa, 1979 Nobel Peace Prize-winner, confronts a particularly stubborn person, she says only that he or she is Jesus in a "distressing disguise." Joy, says Mother Teresa, is the characteristic by which God uses us to re-make the distressing into the desired, the discarded into the creative. "Joy is prayer— Joy is strength—Joy is love—Joy is a net of love by which you can catch souls." The person "gives most who gives with joy." So God takes bad situations and makes them good, and he uses us to help him. He uses us best when we accept our assignments with joy. Test that law for yourself. When you discover its solid truth, your faith will be elevated. That strengthened belief in God's creative faithfulness will gladden your heart and in turn make you God's joyful helper.

Nature and Beauty

A thing of beauty is a joy forever.

—John Keats

*Never lose an opportunity of seeing anything
that is beautiful; for beauty is God's
handwriting—a wayside sacrament. Welcome it
in every fair face, in every fair sky, in every fair
flower, and thank God for it as a cup of blessing.*

—Ralph Waldo Emerson

1
Informality Within Structure

The recent best-seller *In Search of Excellence* reveals that one mark of successful corporations is informality; another mark is structure. Over and again in the book, these twin motifs raise their hands for recognition. Productive management has learned something from nature. There is indeed structure in nature, but it is not rigid. Can you imagine all trees looking alike, all terribly neat with no straggly branches, only straight wood and leaves with strict look-alike coloration?

Have you ever watched ducks dive into a lake? They use the wind currents as slides and, upon hitting the water, see how far they can coast. They are having fun. Such fun, mirth, and humor mark much of nature. And nature is a role model for human beings.

Out of informality, fun and spontaneity arise within a higher framework of order. If the duck spent all her time keeping the ducklings clean and neat, she could not be the unencumbered creature she is. People who overextend the principle of order render themselves disordered and thus quell the very creativity for which they were made.

Throughout *In Search of Excellence,* authors Peters and Waterman state that the highest creativity and best productivity come out of a free and open workplace where management, atmosphere, and even furnishings suggest that *anything* is

179

possible. Companies confined to straight-line procedures have a lower achievement record.

The principle of informality within structure spells excitement. And excitement creates fun, joy, and pride in accomplishment.

2

True Happiness, True Grief

When Paul tells us that death is swallowed up in victory, he quotes the famous Hosea 13:14 passage: "O death, where is thy victory? O grave, where is thy sting?" Then he adds, "The sting of death is sin, and the power of sin is the law. But thanks be to God, who gives us the victory through our Lord Jesus Christ" (1 Cor. 15:54–57). This statement is typical of the death passages in the New Testament, and we stand amazed that joy is their hallmark. Yes, death is seen as an enemy, and it is the occasion for grief, but the divinity in death is so real, so authentic, that Christians find themselves rejoicing.

Paul Tournier, referring to his late wife, Nelly, says, "I can truly say that I have a great grief and that I am a happy man." He confessed that he missed most their times of meditation, that prior to her death he sometimes forgot his private devotional period, but since her homegoing he had not missed a single day. In those times of spiritual focus, Dr. Tournier felt the nearness of his wife.

This sense of closeness is common. Norman Vincent Peale tells about it in *Plus* magazine (March 1985), in the article "When Loved Ones Leave Us." He also spells this out in *Treasury of Joy and Enthusiasm*; and in his autobiography, *The True Joy of Positive Living*, he even refers to a laughter experience at a funeral!

One of the most interesting phenomena Christians face is laughter in the presence of death. This is more than release of tension; it is recognition of what God built into us—the fact of heaven, a place where no tears or evil can exist. Peter Berger believes the comic is heaven breaking through. When my friend Ralph Turnbull died, I realized contentment and deep joy from the moment the word came to me by phone. The reason is clear enough: Ralph now lives in heaven.

Freud hit on something more profound than he may have known when he said, "We can lose nothing without replacing it." That is a law of nature. Nothing can really be destroyed; it may take another shape, but ultimately it resurrects in new life. So the land around Mount St. Helens has already sprouted rich vegetation, despite the recent volcanic eruptions.

The knowledge of resurrection, new life, heaven, is a strong basis for holy hilarity.

3

Nature's Joy

The Living Bible renders the last paragraph of Psalm 65 (vv. 6–13) with immense joy. In verse 8: "The dawn and sunset shout for joy!" Verses 11–12: "Then he crowns it all with green, lush pastures in the wilderness; hillsides blossom with joy." The paragraph's close: "All the world shouts with joy, and sings."

Charles Spurgeon picked up on Scripture's joy in nature when he wrote, "Doth not all nature around me praise God? If I were silent, I should be an exception to the universe." John Burroughs, the naturalist, says that if he had to name the three chief resources of life, they would be books, friends, and nature. He adds that for him the greatest of these is nature, that "at least the most constant and always at hand, is nature." He says more: Nature "moves the heart, appeals to the mind, and fires the imagination—health to the body, a stimulus to the intellect, and joy to the soul." Burroughs explains: "To the scientist, nature is a storehouse of facts, laws, processes; to the artist she is a storehouse of pictures; to the poet she is a storehouse of images, fancies, a source of inspiration; to the moralist she is a storehouse of precepts and parables; to all she may be a source of knowledge and joy."

Even though blind and deaf since infancy, Helen Keller could pen a poem entitled "In the Garden of the Lord," and in that poem she shapes this remarkable line: "I laugh and shout for life is good." The same spirit controlled Elizabeth

Barrett Browning's pen when she wrote: "Earth's crammed with heaven,/And every common bush afire with God.

The eighteenth-century evangelicals saw nature as God's signature. Autographs say something about personality, and God's signature tells us He loves us. Otherwise why give us all this beauty? To see love and beauty in nature is to know true joy. In turn we want to praise the Creator.

4

God Cares
for the Birds

Jesus said, "Look at the birds of the air: they neither sow nor reap nor gather into barns, and yet your heavenly Father feeds them . . ." (Matt. 6:26). God seems to take special delight in taking care of His own. The birds, yes—and us, too.

We have a bird feeder in our back yard near the kitchen windows, from which we can observe our feathered friends. We sometimes laugh at the blue jays; their size and cocky manner make smaller birds fly away—except for cardinals. They carry brilliant color, and they claim their rights!

After the blue jays and cardinals have their feed, the sparrows and finches return. In the end, all get enough to eat.

"Nature is man's religious book," declared Theodore Parker, "with lessons for every day." One lesson we cannot overlook is that God takes care of us.

And there is another lesson, too: birds don't give up easily. They come again and again to the feeder, no matter how formidable the opposition. "All problems become smaller if you don't dodge them but confront them," according to William Halsey. He goes on: "Touch a thistle timidly, and it pricks you; grasp it boldly, and its spines crumble."

Freedom and laughter, a certain bold delight in life, accompany the courage to beard the lion in his den. Timidity, paralysis, and lack of humor go together and rob one of victory-over-the-thistle. Can you even imagine a bird, discouraged and lying down on the job? We can only see birds energetically taking God at his word. Their joy in life is evident for all to see and hear.

> By shallow rivers, to whose falls,
> Melodious birds sing madrigals.
>   —Christopher Marlowe

5

Stars

Job heard God use these words: ". . . when the morning stars sang together, and all the sons of God shouted for joy" (Job 38:7). Nature brings its own joy and therapy. W. H. Auden told us that parents have a duty to teach their children the lessons of nature. Nature's creatures have their own identity, he observed, and can never lose their identities, "because they can only be what they already are: the flowers 'fresh and laughing as on the days of great battles,' the beasts who 'walk the earth, ignorant, while their splendor lasts, of any weakness,' and, most of all," concludes the great writer, "the stars of the night sky, in all their unchanging majesty and stateliness of movement."

Astronomer Johannes Kepler, viewing the heavens, saw star clusters at night and cried, "O God, I think thy thoughts after thee." The magnificence of the night sky recaptures our perspective about God, restores our relationship with Him, and puts joy in our hearts. Why would it not? After all, this Being who could create and manage such a universe can only put fresh strength and renewed motivation into us.

William Beebe, the naturalist, used to visit fellow nature-lover Theodore Roosevelt. Of an evening, after good conversation at Sagamore Hill, Roosevelt's home, the two walked on the lawn, looked up at the stars, and then one or the other would go through their customary ritual:

That is the Spiral Galaxy of Andromeda.
It is as large as our Milky Way.
It is one of a hundred million galaxies.
It is 750,000 light-years away.
It consists of one hundred billion suns,
   each larger than our sun.

Then followed silence. Finally Teddy Roosevelt would say, "Now I think we are small enough. Let's go to bed."

The great God has his ways of showing strength, of communicating goodness, truth, and beauty. The moral obligation within and the starry heavens above speak with peculiar eloquence. To be reminded of this brings a deep settled peace, which is also joy.

6

Give

Jesus told us to "give, and it will be given to you; good measure, pressed down, shaken together, running over, will be put into your lap. For the measure you give will be the measure you get back" (Luke 6:38). This law of life is illustrated in nature. She is always giving and forever receiving.

Jesus also asked us to lend, expecting nothing in return. Nature never calculates the cost of her giving; she just gives—and returns come spontaneously. "Blessed are those who can give without remembering," declared Elizabeth Bibesco, "and take without forgetting." Elton Trueblood came to the heart of joy's dynamic when he announced, "A man has made at least a start on discovering the meaning of human life when he plants shade trees under which he knows full well he will never sit."

Calculated giving ends in sorrow and sadness, cynicism and criticism; but uncomputed giving, by its very nature, yields gladness.

The ancient Maimonides created "The Golden Ladder of Giving," which shows the steps in our potential growth toward liberated, joyful giving:

1. To give reluctantly, the gift of the hand, but not of the heart.
2. To give cheerfully, but not in proportion to need.

189

3. To give cheerfully and proportionately, but not until solicited.
4. To give cheerfully, proportionately, and unsolicited, but to put the gift into the poor man's hand, thus creating shame.
5. To give in such a way that the distressed may know their benefactor, without being known to him.
6. To know the objects of our bounty, but remain unknown to them.
7. To give so that the benefactor may not know those whom he has relieved, and they shall not know him.
8. To prevent poverty by teaching a trade, setting a man up in business, or in some other way preventing the need of charity.

Dear Lord, rob me of all selfishness, and in its place put the generosity that expects nothing but accepts with gratitude and joy everything you send. *Amen.*

7
Truth, Beauty, and Freedom

When Jesus announced that he was the way, the truth, and the life, he made clear for all time the chief source of happiness. For to know the truth is to find freedom. And to discover truth is to open one's eyes to beauty:

> Beauty is truth, truth beauty,—that is all
> Ye know on earth, and all ye need to
> know.
> —John Keats

Legalism will not open one to truth and beauty. How right was John Baillie, the Scottish theologian, when he said, "The New Testament does not say, 'You shall know the rules, and by them you shall be bound,' but, 'You shall know the truth, and the truth shall make you free.'" Joy degenerates in prison; happiness multiplies in freedom. And only truth can make us free.

"Knowledge is happiness," said Helen Keller, "because to have knowledge—broad deep knowledge—is to know true ends from false, and lofty things from low." Learn the benchmarks of human progress, she counsels. Then you will "feel the great heart-throbs" of the centuries. And if one does sense these pulsations? One hears heaven's harmonies and sees earth's potentialities.

Learn truth. It will open your eyes and liberate them to see beauty everywhere. Take, for example, the truth about humor. Astonishing is its omission in most books on management, in nearly all volumes on health, virtually every tome on theology. But those who learn the simple truth that things go better with laughter have opened themselves to a quality and beauty in relationships that will facilitate commerce and health and enhance all living.

Of course, the prior and basic truth is Jesus Christ Himself. And how wondrous is the freedom that goes with the beauty in Christ? Well, Samuel Rutherford made joyous freedom known as vividly as anyone could: "Jesus Christ came into my prison cell last night, and every stone flashed like a ruby." And there you have the practical benefit of the wisdom that has power to emancipate any circumstances and adorn any setting.

Children, Youth, and Family

A happy family is but an earlier heaven.

—John Bowring

1

Do Not
Be Afraid

"But the angel said to him, 'Do not be afraid, Zechariah . . . your wife Elizabeth will bear you a son . . .'" (Luke 1:13).

"And the angel said to her, 'Do not be afraid . . . you will bear a son . . .'" (Luke 1:30–31).

"And the angel said to them [the shepherds], 'Be not afraid; for behold, I bring you good news of a great joy . . . to you is born . . . a Savior . . .'" (Luke 2:10–11).

Fear robs us of mirth and joy; the Savior robs us of fear. He does this through his presence. And he comes in a thousand ways—for example, in little children.

Children, nonthreatening in manner, possess sheer magic for putting us at ease. Their carefree spirit of innocence has nothing of adult calculation about it. Adult cleverness and design make us uneasy. The unalloyed motivations of little children sometimes carry right over into adulthood, and when we meet such a person we often stand amazed, and always we feel tranquil and comfortable.

A university professor sought to itemize reasons people buy:

1. Some make purchases on a *rational* basis, saying, "I need this because. . . ."
2. Others procure merchandise for *emotional* reasons.

195

3. Still others obtain things out of *social pressure*. Subteens and teens especially respond to "what everybody's got."
4. Some shop out of *curiosity*. A new item may bring a certain amount of personal satisfaction.
5. Many procure commodities because of the *situation*— Christmas, a birthday, Mother's Day.

Clearly we live in a world of adult manipulation, a money-oriented environment. That strikes fear to our hearts, for we can never prepare fully for the subtleties invading our lives. Aside from people who try to outwit us, we also fear that the forces of nature or gravity, in storm or accident, will rob us of quality of life, indeed of life itself.

The Christ child came to put those fears to rest. He is the Savior, Immanuel ("God with us"). And when we are around little children anywhere, we experience the non-menacing and affirming presence we were meant for.

Children, like Christ, bring not fear but joy unbounded.

2
Children Make
Us Laugh

Jesus loved little children. No doubt one reason was their natural ability to bring pleasantry into the flow of life. One suspects Jesus had the ability to remove the restraints from children so they could be themselves. We are fortunate to live in an age unlike earlier eras that announced, "Children are to be seen and not heard."

Don Edwards, a newspaper columnist, writes of the little fellow standing at the bottom of a department-store escalator. Intently looking at the handrail, the small boy would not take his eyes away. A salesperson asked, "Are you lost?"— "Nope," came the reply, "I'm waiting for my chewing gum to come back."

The creativity reflected in that little guy, psychologists and researchers now believe, is more significant than raw I.Q. as a measure of intelligence. Getzels and Jackson, University of Chicago psychology professors, did a study that brought them to this conclusion: giftedness is not really "intelligence," but creativity. That's not all: "The outstanding characteristic of the creative child is a sense of humor." Wit and creativity are bedfellows.

Studies involving children and laughter reveal some interesting facts. Babies often laugh first around the tenth week, sometimes earlier. At that age laughter is pretty much reflexive, so their mirthful responses come with surprises and relief. By the sixteenth week, they are laughing out loud on an hourly basis. One of the most interesting findings is that children learn to translate discomfort, stress, and awkward situations into laughter—especially if their parents see the funny side of difficulty. That's one reason young children refresh us so. They model laughter as tension-release, the very thing adults ought to do but frequently avoid! By age four, little ones laugh about every four minutes, usually in the context of their own games, dances, and songs.

A British psychologist, David Cohen, discovered that some sounds and touches can trigger laughter between four and six months. He found that by the tenth month, visual and social stimuli can set infants laughing—for example, when Mother crawls on the floor! The end of the first year sees children making some of their own fun, inventing their own fantasies. Peek-a-boo, modeled by parents, now takes hold of the child's imagination; he or she may peer around the sofa. At about one year, the child can burlesque, slapping himself on the thigh and pretending, for example, that he is a TV cartoon figure.

Even preschoolers have been known to use humor as a self-critical device. Evidently it also doesn't take long for children to learn to play "sneak" with humor. Wasn't it Freud who observed that jokes can be subtle aggression against authority figures?

3

Laughter as
an Instrument
of Maturation

Evidently Jesus' lest-ye-become-as-a-little-child principle reflects more than a humble and open spirit. In fact, the spin-offs are too great to count. But recent research seems to indicate that maturation is one of those by-products, and humor aids the process.

Someone has called catecholamines "alertness hormones." We have already seen that catecholamines, by triggering endorphins (the body's natural painkillers), can reduce aches, discomfort, inflammation, and so on. We also know that the brain's receptors open up to enhance learning. Relaxation sets in, and that, too, frees the mind for instruction. Laughter is a practical instrument for education and important to the maturation process.

This relaxation response in laughter has undergone considerable research. Some findings: the greater and longer the laugh, the more uptightness diminishes. Tension reduction is a major challenge in the learning/maturation enterprise.

Children like riddles; older young people prefer jokes. Both age groups try their growing vocabulary of words and ideas on older folk to get feedback, which can nurture emotional and cognitive growth. Adults usually tell stories with puns and subtle punch lines, a much more sophisticated genre of humor. So humor sharing becomes a method of learning in the younger, and in adults is evidence that mastery has arrived.

Sobriety seems to set in at about middle age, unless individuals program themselves otherwise. Evidently the increased burdens of life tend to diminish the comic elements in our personalities. After retirement the laughter comes back a little, especially in our seventies and eighties. This probably relates to newfound relief from the daily round of responsibilities, coupled with the leisure to see the funny things people do.

But, at any age, one function of laughter seems to be the signaling of wholesome self-regard. And a strong self-image relates closely to what we know as human maturity.

By the way, some research seems to indicate that positive and affirmative facts and experiences return to memory much better if one smiles or laughs. Contrariwise, smiling does not seem to have this recall effect on negative details.

4

Communicating Faith in our Families

That delightful woman Phyllis McGinley writes somewhere that in the canonization process, the Catholic Church requires proof of joy in the candidate. She admits she cannot cite chapter and verse, but I like the suggestion that sourness is not a sacred attribute.

It is said of that mighty spirit, "Praying Hyde" of India, that he was known for two things: the effectiveness of his intercessions and the hilarity of his laugh. Could the two be related?

Faith is contagious. I am convinced that the gift of faith is more apt to be accepted when it is evidenced in those around us. I am also convinced that children, by nature, avoid someone whose Spartan rigor is not balanced by laughter and the lighter side of life.

Psalm 126:2 has the mark of authenticity about it: "Then our mouth was filled with laughter, and our tongue with shouts of joy; then they said among the nations, 'The LORD has done great things for them.'" G. K. Chesterton announced profound truth when he exclaimed, "Joy, which was the small publicity of the pagan, is the gigantic secret of the Christian." It is that gigantic secret our families look for today. Indeed, everyone searches for it. For it is the secret of life abundant, what everybody wants.

Families know (learn) by our demeanor that the real values

in life are not houses, lands, and things—they are instruments. But for contact with reality, they must "see" in the biblical sense. Laughter is one of God's ways of uncovering reality.

Currently, the four leading causes of death in our culture are high blood pressure, heart disease, stroke, and cancer. Stress has been implicated in each. We know, for example, that stress worsens these diseases. If laughter, pleasantry, and affirming thoughts contribute to prevention and alleviation of illness, we have a degree of therapy at our fingertips. And when we take advantage of this healing power, we project the life of faith to our households.

Whenever faith finds creative and positive expression, know this: its nature is contagion. Holy contagion!

5

Dropping Cares

Psalm 94:19 reads: "When the cares of my heart are many, thy consolations cheer my soul." And in 1 Peter 5:7 we are told to cast our anxieties on God because he cares for us.

Have you heard the story of the two Japanese monks? Traveling a muddy road, a downpour only added to the difficulty of walking. Around a bend in the road, they met a lovely girl in flowing silk kimono, unable to cross the intersection. One monk, Tanzan, immediately took the girl in his arms and carried her through the mud and onto more secure ground.

The monks continued their hike, but the other monk, Ekido, spoke not a word until they reached their temple lodgings that night. Now he restrained himself no longer: "We monks never go near females," he remonstrated with Tanzan, "most particularly not young and pretty ones." Ekido had to say more: "It is dangerous, so why did you do it?"

"I left the girl there," replied Tanzan in a quiet spirit. "Are *you* still carrying her?"

The touch of humor in that little story rings with wisdom. Unloading cares and temptations, decisions past and future, comes a lot easier with a bit of glee.

Simon Tugwell, who tells the story of the two monks, indicates that "we must learn to pass through situations like a fish, rather than carrying them all with us like a snail." A too-intense attention to life's experiences can drain spirit and emotions. To nurture the art of unloading, without shirking responsibility, is a significant secret of happy living.

Why carry more with us than we need to? Each life event carries quite enough challenge by itself! This is especially relevant to our family life, for there we have our chief investment and intensity mounts quickly.

Good news: God will help us cast our cares on him because he cares for us.

6

Antidote
to Cynicism

"When he entered the house," according to Matthew 9:28, "the blind men came to him; and Jesus said to them, 'Do you believe that I am able to do this?' They said to him, 'Yes, Lord.'" Indeed, belief is the vehicle for healing, and cynicism is its worst enemy.

There is an unhealthy laughter that fosters distrust and reinforces doubt. Tragically, it is this very laughter that can ultimately destroy laughter itself. But that need not be the case. Attitude is a choice.

Marian Diamond, of the University of California, discovered that we human beings never fully outgrow our childhood. Children believe naturally, whereas cynicism is an adult accretion. So we have nature on our side to help us decide for belief.

Diamond discovered from her research that we need never stop learning. We can always submit to needed and progressive change if we will. Perhaps best of all, we can decide to keep laughing.

One of the key factors in nudging us to decide for childlike belief—to choose to learn, change, and laugh—is what is modeled in the home. As kids grow to adulthood and have to wrestle with the hassles of life, cynicism has an insidious way of taking hold. Disappointments, reverses, and difficulties can produce a defeatist mind-set, especially if negativism has characterized one's homelife in the early years. That, in turn, often yields the stinking flower called burnout. But Freudenberger and North, in their book *Women's Burnout,* make an interesting observation: "Very few people suffer burnout when they're having fun." The two researchers summarize twelve ways to avoid burnout, and the twelfth is to nurture and maintain your sense of humor.

If cynicism can easily become habitual, so can wholesome laughter. And the latter is more contagious than the former! More, a spirit of fun possesses the capacity to halt cynicism in its earliest stages.

7

Best Friends

"A good wife who can find?" asks the writer of Proverbs 31. "She is far more precious than jewels" (v. 10). The next verse gives a reason: "The heart of her husband trusts in her." And there is the basis of the most intimate friendship, the friendship we call marriage.

Later in that remarkable chapter of Proverbs, which hails the hallmarks of the good wife, the writer says "she laughs at the time to come" (v. 25). She does not worry about tomorrow; she can laugh because strength and dignity clothe her, because she tackles the duties of life with courage and forthrightness. Whatever happens, this woman is prepared to face it.

Francis Bacon observed that "There is no man that imparteth his joys to his friends, but he joyeth the more; and no man that imparteth his griefs to his friend, but he grieveth the less." The same holds true with husband and wife, with children and parents. Confrontation with life in the family unit requires genuine love, and joy is the child of love.

When this kind of honest-to-goodness friendship exists in the family, what other members do has a way of carrying interest and excitement. Crafts and projects, money tallying and usage, yard care and house maintenance, meal preparation and cleaning up after eating—all have about them the earmark of mutual effort and the sense of joyous reward.

The family's eating experiences can be enriched by the joy

of storytelling, sharing the day's events, wholesome give-and-take in the grand enterprise of learning, joking, and ribbing of one another. All these little love signs spell warmth and deep joy and bring peace and well-being.

William Hazlitt rightly said we cannot force friendship any more than we can force love. But we do know some things that will foster friendship and love in the family. We can focus on Christ, the source of joy; we can concentrate on positive experiences. Even when we must empty our souls of negatives, the family can listen with support. And affirmation blossoms into joy.

Families that cultivate one another as best friends also reflect God's available grace for creating peace and joy.

Sources for the Renewal of Joy

For, lo, the winter is past, the rain is over and gone; The flowers appear on the earth; the time of the singing of birds is come, and the voice of the turtle is heard in our land.

—Song of Solomon 2:11–12 (KJV)

1

The Primary Source

In Psalm 100, replete with joy, we read in the New International Version:

> Shout for joy to the LORD, all the earth.
> Serve the LORD with gladness;
>   come before him with joyful songs.
> Know that the LORD is God.
>   It is he who made us, and we are his;
>   we are his people, the sheep of his pasture.
> Enter his gates with thanksgiving
>   and his courts with praise;
>   give thanks to him and praise his name.
> For the LORD is good and his love endures forever;
>   his faithfulness continues through all generations.

In that exuberant piece of poetry we have the secrets of renewed joy.

The first secret lies in the knowledge that the Lord is God. The ancient writer Marcianus Aristides observed that "God is not in need of anything, but all things are in need of him." God is supreme, God is in charge of everything, God is Creator. The sure knowledge that God *is* God is the primary source of security and, therefore, of renewed joy.

The second great secret comes on the heels of the first: God is good. Lady Julian of Norwich saw the relationship between the two secrets: "Some of us believe that God is Almighty

211

and may do all, and that he is All-wisdom and can do all; but that he is All-love and will do all—there we stop short." God is indeed good. Good, mind you, not merely in theory, but in terms of his involvement in the world, in you and me, and in all his children. That good, says our psalm, endures forever. Put in practical language, God's faithfulness goes on from generation to generation.

One further truth about this psalm is that it is couched in a spirit of unadulterated thankfulness. Said Izaak Walton, "God has two dwellings—one in heaven and the other in a thankful heart." Well now, since God cannot possibly be divorced from joy, the heart that has him owns gladness.

How to be renewed in joy? Seek God and find him.

2

Suffering and Joy

The apostle Paul, in one of his soaring moments, declared, "No, in all these things we are more than conquerors through him who loved us. For I am sure that neither death, nor life, nor angels, nor principalities, nor things present, nor things to come, nor powers, nor height, nor depth, nor anything else in all creation, will be able to separate us from the love of God in Christ Jesus our Lord" (Rom. 8:37–39).

Here Paul triumphs over tragedy. He never once tries to avoid the hard fact of suffering. Indeed, he seems to see it as opportunity to overcome with zest. Humor and joy often come out of raw suffering. Sincere laughter and authentic joy relate to all of life, including hardship.

You will notice immediately that Paul does not entertain fears of suffering. Said a wise man, "What is unbearable is not to suffer but to be afraid of suffering." Fearful persons, as in athletic experiences, miss half the game and thereby rob themselves of fulfillment and joy.

To accept suffering as part of life is a great freedom. That leads us to another liberating truth, one couched by Simone Weil, the French mystic: "It is in affliction itself that the splendour of God's mercy shines. . . ." Mother Teresa knows this truth, for she says that God is closest to the poorest of the poor. Jesus talked about the blessedness, the happiness, of the poor in spirit. Baron von Hugel saw this clearly when he

213

said, "Suffering is the great teacher." He even says we have our value system all wrong, that "suffering is the crown of life." He explains: "Suffering and expansion [another term for education], what a rich combination!" Von Hugel goes on: "All deepened life is deepened suffering, deepened dreariness, deepened joy. Suffering and joy. The final note of religion is joy."

Suffering refines us, peels off the layers of selfishness, shoves us into a hurting world to mend its wounds, and above all teaches us something of the meaning of the cross of Christ. When all that begins to take shape in our thinking, we find ourselves. Alexander Solzhenitsyn said of his experience in the Russian prison camp that there he discovered his soul. He, like Paul, could thank God for suffering. This accounts for the joy in both men.

3

Growing Faith

Saint Paul's personal joy overflows as he addresses the Christians at Thessalonica: "We are bound to give thanks to God always for you, brethren, as is fitting, because your faith is growing abundantly, and the love of every one of you for one another is increasing" (2 Thess. 1:3). He goes on to talk about "faith in all your persecutions and in the afflictions which you are enduring" (v. 4). Clearly these early Christians were growing in that all-important life component, faith.

This is a tricky business, for the world conditions us to believe that happiness is in mere pleasure, the transitory, the sensual. Although those things can possess potential for good, raw worldly gratification is a dead-end street. This is why William Wordsworth, in *The Prelude*, is at pains to say:

> Not in Utopia,—subterranean fields,—
> Or some secreted island, Heaven knows where!
> But in the very world, which is the world
> Of all of us,—the place where, in the end,
> We find our happiness, or not at all!

In other words, authentic gladness comes from within yourself. Put more fully, it stems from sturdy, developing faith.

Mary Asquith helps us think clearly about faith: "There is a difference between a good, sound reason for our faith, and a reason that sounds good." Shallow faith, like a tree rotted inside, blows over in the storms of persecution and affliction.

215

Even the classic writers about Utopia seemed to have understood this. The very word *utopia* means "no place." William Norris did a book called *News From Nowhere,* but Samuel Butler did one called *Erehwon,* NOWHERE spelled backwards.

Jesus said the kingdom of God (faith) is in us (Luke 17:21) and that it had come with Him. The source of true happiness is His kingdom. When that kingdom lives in us by Christ's Spirit, faith reigns.

That faith, that kingdom of joy, needs periodic refurbishing. How do we do that? "We are not called upon to renew our minds in order that we may be transfigured," said William L. Pettingill; "we are only to yield ourselves unto God, and he does all the rest." And what is this "all the rest?" Ah! Christopher Morley had it right: "April prepares her green traffic light and the world thinks go." Temple Gairdner talked well of renewal's reality: "That sense of newness is simply delicious. It makes new the Bible and friends, and all mankind and love and spiritual things and Sunday and church and God himself." Now that's real joy!

4

Fulfilling Work

The Book of Proverbs tells us that we should "commit" our work "to the LORD"; then our "plans will be established" (Prov. 16:3). That is a way of saying that when we labor with noble purpose to achieve something worthwhile, we experience deep satisfaction and real joy.

That is the way my friend Dr. Kenneth Kinghorn feels after completing a writing project, even one unit of a project. If, he says, he can end a workday knowing he has been productive, that's about as good a feeling as he ever comes by. And the completion of a whole book brings decided gratification.

The clue to that sense of well-being comes from committing your work "to the Lord." As Martin Luther observed, "A dairymaid can milk cows to the glory of God." Once one believes his or her efforts center in honoring God, pride in quality productivity enters the soul. George MacDonald, that unusual Scottish storyteller who influenced C. S. Lewis, remarked that "It is our best work that he [God] wants, not the dregs of our exhaustion. I think he must prefer quality to quantity." There you have one of the big secrets of fulfillment, for we intuitively know that excellence supersedes mere quantity. We know that well, despite our emphasis on mass production and the planned obsolescence that goes with a high-tech economy.

Quality demands hard work. Not joyless labor, but diligence. One writer revises his text a dozen times. The rule of thumb in journalistic circles is five, but he will not be satisfied with ordinary editing. Michelangelo called details "trifles" and then unobserved that "perfection is no trifle." "If people knew how hard I work to get my mastery," he once said, "it wouldn't seem so wonderful after all." But, oh! how wonderful it really is to aim for quality. And how extraordinary any person's creativity is in God's sight when done with care.

Somehow the knowledge of God's approval gives us that special kick we get out of exertion. William Lyon Phelps, Yale professor of English, used to say he wished he could pay for the privilege of teaching. Walter Muelder, long-time dean of Boston University Divinity School, said his work was just plain fun. When work is fun it rejuvenates, contributes to wholeness, and points to God.

The bottom line: work itself can renew joy in the human spirit.

5

Leisure and Creative Experience

Jesus announced truth with unsurpassed beauty and meaning. On one occasion He gave this counsel: "Come to me, all who labor and are heavy laden, and I will give you rest. Take my yoke upon you, and learn from me; for I am gentle and lowly in heart, and you will find rest for your souls. For my yoke is easy, and my burden is light" (Matt. 11:28–30). Edgar W. Howe, putting his finger on one of the ways we rob ourselves of joy, said, "It's no credit to anyone to work too hard." Any attempt to project feelings of the "heavy laden" syndrome falls short of God's will.

An important source of joy is taking time off so we can return to work with zest, enthusiasm, and purpose. The trick is to put experiences of creative substance in those periodic times of refreshment. Some will go to a bookstore. Not a bad idea, for in a really good one the browser surveys an art gallery in miniature. Even modern book jackets reflect a whole genre of creative expression. Children's books take us into an art world of their own, a world that says we live in a renaissance of children's literature and drawing. The classics section of the store reminds us of hope and idealism and thus restores our faith in God, others, and life itself. The very arrangement of the books by sections, the overall visual impact, has in itself a renewing effect. Books are friends that invigorate us.

Some will migrate not to a bookstore but to a concert and get their fill of great music, silver-toned sounds with power to restore the soul. Others will go out into nature—to a park for a picnic, to the wilderness to hunt, to the mountains to watch God paint His sunsets. Still others will join friends with mutual interests at a dinner party, where the talk and good food play their revitalizing roles.

Workaholism is a thief, a deceiver who wears the mask of joy. Periodic leisure, filled with good things, restores one's imaginative powers, making the daily round not just bearable but exalted with true dignity and joyous reality.

6

Friends

The Book of Proverbs has a way of couching truth in but a few words. For example, "A friend loves at all times, and a brother is born for adversity" (Prov. 17:17). Samuel Johnson, in his inimitable way, declared, "If a man does not make new acquaintances as he advances through life, he will soon find himself left alone. A man, sir, should keep his friendship in constant repair." The necessity for friends finds documentation in the very flow of life. Few joys surpass friendship. Essays, indeed whole books, have been written on the subject.

No research is more eloquent than the recent study of 7,000 people who suffered such cataclysmic diseases as cancer or vascular problems. Recorded in the *American Journal of Epidemiology*, the essential finding is this: those who enjoyed a strong support system of friends and family survived at a much higher rate than those without such a system. We know some of the reasons for that, since friends bring joy and enthusiasm, a certain verve and pizzazz characterized by stories, laughter, and general well-being. All that, we also know, kicks antibodies into action, enhancing the endocrine and hormonal systems to stave off or even reverse disease. In other words, the support system created by friends and family activates the body's own therapy and support systems.

The source of friendship is God. An amazing passage in the Old Testament reads: "Thus the LORD used to speak to Moses face to face, as a man speaks to his friend . . ." (Exod.

33:11). That kind of relationship with God fosters therapy and guidance. And once that fundamental relationship is established, human friends come naturally, for people migrate toward the wholesomeness God engenders. Charles F. Andrews bears testimony to the power of friendship with God: "The older I grow in years, the more the wonder and the joy increase when I see the power of these words of Jesus—'I have called you friends'—to move the human heart. That one word 'friend' breaks down each barrier of reserve, and we have boldness in his presence." He concludes: "Our hearts go out in love to meet his love." That love defines the wholesomeness that brings friends.

Now, then, who can possibly know the love of God and human friends and be destitute of joy?

7

The Retreat Experience

Psalm 116:7 reads: "Return, O my soul, to your rest; for the LORD has dealt bountifully with you." The word *rest* occurs frequently in Scripture. God rested on the seventh day; Jesus invited his friends to come away to rest; the Book of Hebrews is filled with the concept; and we find it in Genesis, Exodus, and other places.

The function of a retreat is rest, the restoration of mind and body along with the spiritual and emotional refurbishing that comes in a well-thought-out program. Fortunately we live in an age of opportunities for spiritual renewal. Leaving telephone, mailbox, office, daily routine, paves the way for opening the soul to fresh messages from God, self, and others. These dispatches flow with astonishing frequency once we quiet ourselves to listen.

Henry Vaughan, seventeenth-century writer, captures the therapy of retreat under the figure of night:

> Dear Night! this world's defeat;
> The stop to busy fools; care's check and curb;
> The day of spirits; my soul's calm retreat
> Which none disturb!

The absence of that undisturbed calm issues inevitably in the draining off of joy. And the reverse is true: the inspiration of silence restores the glad heart.

But we must know how to use silence. Thus the necessity of the well-structured retreat. We must have leaders who can stimulate our minds with probing questions and comforting, strengthening commentary on life. We must have group sharing that invites the Spirit of God to wash over our souls like green fields and still waters. And the pace and periods between talk must be sufficient to permit that cleansing refreshment.

Retreats do not cost very much, but the interest on the investment is a hundredfold. Encourage yourself to attend the next available retreat. Work toward such a program in your church and community. Stir enthusiasm after a spiritual getaway by offering public witness to its benefits. With retreat centers covering the nation, leaders in abundance, experts on "camping," the specialist knowledge we now possess about small-group dynamics, and the wide range of themes for spiritual encounter—well, the sky's the limit! And unbounded, too, is the renewed joy that retreats can bring.

Bibliography

Allen, Steve. *How to Make A Speech*. New York: McGraw-Hill, 1986.
_____. *Funny People*. New York: Stein and Day, 1981.
Armour, Richard. *It All Started with Freshman English*. New York: McGraw-Hill, 1973.
Barclay, William. *Daily Celebration*. Vol. 2. Edited by Denis Duncan. Waco, Tex.: Word Books, 1974.
Barnes, John. "Politicians and Comics Share Laughs." *The Grand Rapids Press*, September 19, 1986, 1.
Basset, Elizabeth, ed. *Love Is My Meaning: An Anthology of Assurance*. Foreword by Her Majesty Queen Elizabeth the Queen Mother. Atlanta: John Knox Press, 1974.
"Becoming Fools for Christ: Clowning as an Aid to Holy Ritual and Service." *Time*, September 1, 1980.
Berger, Peter. *A Rumor of Angels*. Garden City: Doubleday, 1969.
Bishop, George. *The World of Clowns*. Los Angeles: Brooke House, 1976.
Book of Common Prayer. New York: Harper, 1944.
Brengle, Samuel Logan. *Resurrection Life and Power*. Atlanta: The Salvation Army Supplies and Purchasing Dept., 1981 reprint.
_____. *Helps to Holiness*. Atlanta: The Salvation Army Supplies and Purchasing Dept., 1981 reprint.
Brody, Robert. "Anatomy of a Laugh." *American Health*, November/December 1983.
Buffington, Perry W. "Make 'Em Laugh." *Sky*, April 1984.
Bullock, Alan, and Stallybrass, Oliver, eds. *The Harper Dictionary of Modern Thought*. New York: Harper, 1977.
Burns, George. *How to Live to Be 100—or More*. New York: G. P. Putnam's Sons, 1983.

Buscaglia, Leo. *Loving Each Other: The Challenge of Human Relationships.* New York: Holt, Rinehart and Winston, 1944.

"Clown College." *National Geographic World,* September 1982.

Collins, Susan. "Ford's Stairway Slip Given a Papal Halo." *The Grand Rapids Press,* September 19, 1986, A 5.

Cousins, Norman. *Anatomy of an Illness as Perceived by the Patient.* New York: W. W. Norton and Co., 1979.

Demaray, Donald E., *Watch Out for Burnout.* Grand Rapids: Baker Book House, 1983.

Donahue, Phil. *The Human Animal.* New York: Simon and Schuster, 1985.

Douglas, John A. "Ford's Gala's Top of the Line." *The Grand Rapids Press,* September 19, 1986, B 1.

Edwards, Don. "Bright Christmas." *Lexington [Kentucky] Herald-Leader,* December 19, 1985, B 1.

Elias, Marilyn. "Be Upbeat and Beat Illness, Stress." *USA Today,* August 26, 1985, D 1.

Esar, Evan. *Esar's Comic Dictionary.* Garden City: Doubleday, 1983.

Farris, John T. *The Book of Joy.* London: Hodder and Stoughton, 1917.

Freudenberger, Herbert J., and North, Gail. *Women's Burnout.* Garden City: Doubleday, 1985.

Fry, William F., Jr., and Allen, Melanie. *Make 'em Laugh: Life Studies of Comedy Writers.* Palo Alto, Calif.: Science and Behavior Books, 1975.

Fry, William F., Jr. *Sweet Madness: A Study of Humor.* Palo Alto, Calif.: Pacific Books, 1963.

Gaebelein, Frank E. *The Christian, The Arts, and Truth.* Portland, Oreg.: Multnomah Press, 1985.

Gossip, Arthur John. *In The Secret Place of the Most High being Some Studies in Prayer.* London: Independent Press, 1946.

Hall, Clarence W. *Samuel Logan Brengle: Portrait of a Prophet.* Atlanta: The Salvation Army Supplies and Purchasing Dept., 1979 reprint.

Herbert, Sir Alan. "The English Laugh." (The English Association Presidential Address.) Oxford: University Press, 1950.

Hogan, John. "Orben Debunks Perception that Ford Is a Bumbler." *The Grand Rapids Press,* September 19, 1986, A 5.

Jennison, Keith W. *The Humorous Mr. Lincoln.* New York: Bonanza Books, 1965.

Job, Reuben P., and Shawchuck, Norman. eds. *A Guide to Prayer for Ministers and Other Servants.* Nashville: The Upper Room, 1983.

Johnson, Janice. "Laughs Every Day Could Keep the Doctor Away." *USA Weekend,* November 22–24, 1985.

Kidder, Rushworth M. "TV Has Turned Public Discussion into 'Sea of Amusements.'" *Lexington [Kentucky] Herald-Leader,* November 26, 1985, editorial page.

Knille, Robert, ed. *As I Was Saying . . . A Chesterton Reader*. Grand Rapids: Eerdmans, 1985.

LaBelle, Tom. "Off Stage, They're Normally Funny, Naturally." The Grand Rapids Press, September 19, 1986, A 4.

"Laugh Yourself to Health." *The Indianapolis Star*, October 30, 1977, Section 3.

"Laughing Away Dental Fears." *Prevention*, December 1984, p. 9.

"Laughing Toward Longevity." *Wellness Letter*, June 1985. Berkeley: University of California School of Public Health.

"Laughter Heals: Positive Thoughts are A Potent Cure." *The Seattle Times*, May 21, 1983.

"Laughter *Is* the Best Medicine." *Reader's Digest*, April 1985, p. 47.

Layman, Fred D. "Theology and Humor." *The Asbury Seminarian*, Winter 1982–83. Wilmore, Ky.: Asbury Theological Seminary.

Lloyd-Jones, Martyn. *Joy Unspeakable: Power and Renewal in the Holy Spirit*. Edited by Christopher Catherwood. Wheaton, Ill: Harold Shaw, 1984.

McGhee, Paul E., and Goldstein, Jeffrey H. *Handbook of Humor Research*. Vol. 2, *Applied Studies*. New York: Springer-Verlag, 1983.

Meisel, Martin. "Oscar Wilde." *World Book* (Chicago: Field Enterprises Educational Corporation, 1975). Vol. 21, p. 254.

"Members Request for Humor Brought Avalanche of Ideas." *AARP News Bulletin*, April 1985.

Minirth, Frank B., M.D., and Meier, Paul D., M.D. *Happiness Is a Choice: A Manual on the Symptoms, Causes, and Cures of Depression*. Foreword by Paul Tournier. Grand Rapids: Baker Book House, 1978.

Moody, Raymond A., M.D. *Laugh after Laugh: The Healing Power of Humor*. Jackson, Fla: Headwaters Press, 1978.

Morrice, William. *Joy in the New Testament*. Foreword by A. M. Hunter. Grand Rapids: Eerdmans, 1984.

Mullen, Tom. *Laughing Out Loud and Other Religious Experiences*. Waco, Tex.: Word Books, 1983.

Mullen, Wilbur. "Toward a Theology of Humor." *Christian Scholar's Review*, March 1973.

Myra, Harold L. "A Message from the Publisher." *Christianity Today*, December 13, 1985, p. 17.

Oliver, Robert T. *The Psychology of Persuasive Speech*. 2d ed. New York: David McKay, 1957.

Parrott, Bob W. *God's Sense of Humor—Where? When? How?* New York: Philosophical Library, 1984.

Peale, Norman Vincent. *The True Joy of Positive Living: An Autobiography*. Carmel, N.Y.: Guideposts, 1984.

_____. *Treasury of Joy and Enthusiasm*. Pawling, N.Y.: Foundation for Christian Living, 1981.

_____. "When Loved Ones Leave Us." *Plus*, March 1985 (Pawling, N.Y.: Foundation for Christian Living).

Peter, Laurence J. *The Laughter Prescription: How to Achieve Health, Happiness, and Peace of Mind Through Humor*. New York: Ballantine, 1982.

Peters, Thomas J., and Waterman, Robert H., Jr. *In Search of Excellence*. New York: Harper, 1982.

Peterson, Eugene H. *A Long Obedience in the Same Direction*. Downers Grove, Ill.: Inter-Varsity, 1980.

Postman, Neil. *Amusing Ourselves To Death: Public Disclosure in The Age of Showbusiness*. New York: Viking Press, 1985.

Raskin, Victor: "Jokes: A Linguist Explains His New Semantic Theory of Humor." *Psychology Today,* October 1985.

Richie, Charles. "Humor . . . in Christian Living." *Evangelical Beacon,* November 25, 1985.

Rohrer, Norman B. *Leighton Ford: A Life Surprised*. Wheaton: Tyndale House, 1981.

Schlink, Mother Basilea. *Repentance—The Joy-filled Life*. Minneapolis: Bethany House Publishers, 1984.

Sidey, Hugh. "The Wit and Wisdom." *Time,* September 22, 1986, p. 35.

Smith, Jane Stuart, and Carlson, Betty. *A Gift of Music: Great Composers and Their Influence*. Westchester, Ill.: Cornerstone Books, 1979.

Spangler, Ann, ed. *Bright Legacy: Portraits of Ten Outstanding Christian Women*. Ann Arbor, Mich.: Servant Books, 1983.

Teichman, Howard. "The Brave Journey of Helen Hayes." *Parade,* November 24, 1985.

Tournier, Paul. "The Blessings of a Deep Loss." *Christianity Today,* November 23, 1984, pp. 28–9.

Trueblood, Elton. *The Humor of Christ*. New York: Harper, 1975 Jubilee reprint.

Turner, Dale E. "Words of Wisdom and Other Columns." Seattle: *The Seattle Times,* n.d.

Tuttle, Lee F. *Profiles of 20th Century Pulpit Giants: From Personal Acquaintance*. Published in 1984 by the author in Lake Junaluska, N.C.

Wallis, Charles, L., ed. *The Treasure Chest*. New York: Harper, 1965.

Wilde, Oscar. *The Importance of Being Earnest*. Edited by Vincent F. Hopper and Gerald B. Lahey. Woodbury, N.Y.: Barron's Educational Series, n.d.

Wilentz, Amy. "Having the Last Laugh." *Time,* September 22, 1986, p. 32.

———. "Pitfalls of the Presidency." *Time,* September 29, 1986, p. 32.

Will, George F. "Dickens' Emphasis Was on Individual." *Lexington [Kentucky] Herald-Leader,* November 29, 1985.

Woods, Ralph L., compiler. *Friendship*. Norwalk, Conn.: C. R. Gibson, 1969.